S0-BUF-957

A Look Backward and Forward at American Professional Women and their Families

Edited by
Rita J. Simon

University Press of America, Inc.
Lanham • New York • Oxford

University Press of America,® Inc.
4720 Boston Way
Lanham, Maryland 20706

12 Hid's Copse Rd.
Cumnor Hill, Oxford OX2 9JJ

Printed in the United States of America
British Library Cataloging in Publication Information Available

Co-published by arrangement with the
Women's Freedom Network

Library of Congress Cataloging-in-Publication Data

A look backward and forward at American professional women and their families/edited by Rita J. Simon
p. cm.
1. Working mothers—United States—Congresses. 2. Work and family—United States—Congresses. 3. Women in the professions—United States—Congresses. 4. Businesswomen—United States—Congresses. 5. Women Soldiers—United States—Congresses. I. Simon, Rita James.
HQ759.48.L66 1999 305.4—dc21 99—052302 CIP

ISBN 0-7618-1581-3 (cloth: alk. ppr.)
ISBN 0-7618-1582-1 (pbk: alk. ppr.)

™ The paper used in this publication meets the minimum requirements of American National Standard for Information Sciences—Permanence of Paper for Printed Library Materials, ANSI Z39.48—1984

Contents

Introduction

This book is a product of many thoughtful and often inspiring papers presented at the Women's Freedom Network's Fourth Annual Conference in Washington, D.C. on October 18, 1997. Presentations were made by scholars, homemakers, entrepreneurs, professionals, and military personnel addressing the status of women, their careers, and their families—now, and in the past. We found these presentations compelling enough to collect into one book and hope that you will also find them interesting to read and reflect upon. The volume is divided into four major sections, the contents of which are described as follows:

Section One focuses on the American family. It includes three papers that describe the choices successful, professional women have made in managing their professional and personal lives, especially as those choices affect their relationship with their spouses and children. An additional piece discusses the evolving role of fatherhood and the portrayal of men and fathers in the media. Two additional pieces discuss the impact of divorce on children. One of those papers assesses the problem of fatherlessness and the pain children experience when their fathers are physically, financially, or emotionally disconnected. The second piece discusses the benefits of joint custody, as opposed to sole custody, and the resulting impact on child support and development.

In Section Two, four women discuss their successful careers as entrepreneurs and CEOs in a variety of businesses. These women take you back almost twenty years and describe how they got their first bank loan, landed their first client, and began to see their businesses earn a profit. They describe the types of women who came before them and the women they see starting their own businesses today. All of these women have much in common, but the authors are also careful to point out how the economy, society, and the status of women have changed over the years and how those changes are likely to influence the challenges future entrepreneurs will confront.

Women in the military is the focus of the papers in Section Three. Three of the authors are career officers in the Army, the Navy, and the Air Force, respectively. The fourth woman served as a chaplain in the Army. Tension exists between the officers and the chaplain as they discuss and disagree about women's performance in the military. They address issues of physical fitness, injury, non-deployability due to pregnancy, and women's participation in sexual misconduct scandals. The three officers provide a much more positive assessment of women's performance in the military than the chaplain does.

Section Four, the final section, presents women in various professions—comparing their history and experiences, and also the changes that have emerged in each profession. Two pieces present different perspectives on women and how they practice law. Because no woman professors appeared on the panel, I have included a brief account of my experiences as a woman in academia from the 1950s until today. The next two pieces describe the practice of medicine and nursing over a period of four decades, from the 1950s through the 1980s. Finally, two women describe their experiences in journalism, from fifty years ago until today.

Part I

The American Family

In this section, we present six papers that contemplate the evolving role of women and men in the American family. First, three women—Marilyn Mangan, Katherine Kersten, and Jennifer Roback Morse—describe the various choices they have made in their professional and personal lives. Marilyn Mangan reveals the unexpected fulfilment of leaving her high-powered legal and political career to stay home and raise her daughter; Katherine Kersten offers thoughtful insight into the benefits of home schooling and the role of family in education; and Jennifer Roback Morse offers a novel and controversial critique of modern feminism and its effect on the nuclear family. Next, three men—Wade Horn, Ronald Henry, and Armin Brott—each discuss a father's role in today's family life and in society. Wade Horn evaluates the tremendous impact of fatherlessness on our modern society, Ron Henry compares joint custody to sole custody and the effect of each on the children of divorced parents, and finally, Armin Brott discusses generally the image and expectations of fathers today. While you may not agree with all the authors have to say, these six pieces offer an interesting and very personal glimpse into some of the issues and problems faced by families in today's society.

Chapter 1

ᢒᢓ

Transition: From the Senate to the House

MARILYN J. MANGAN*

As I moved away from an identity largely defined by my career to the innate role of wife and mother, I followed a path that many of my friends who preceded me have described as rocky and uncertain. Some of them have repeated to me that one must be strong in order to be secure in one's identity. The converse is to avoid allowing social or other pressures to define your identity for you. I needed to be secure in who I was, because in my new role there is oftentimes not the rewards and the tangible definition of success that I experienced through most of my career.

My career as a lawyer, counsel to non-profit organizations, legislative assistant in the Senate, and international public relations professional over the course of eighteen years took me into the world of diplomats, politicians, and a range of characters with their agendas. This all feels

---

*Marilyn J. Mangan is an attorney. She has worked as counsel to non-profit organizations, legislative assistant in the Senate, and as an international public relations professional.

like the ancient past when I read "Madeleine" bedtime stories to my daughter, Niki. I now have confidential "briefings" at the end of the day when Niki shares her fears, hopes, and questions with me on a range of issues from computer class to guardian angels.

My focus has shifted dramatically from the world of Senate hearings, receptions in the White House Rose Garden, and elaborate dinners at the British Embassy or the Royal Embassy of Saudi Arabia. Now I stick to the friendly confines of the laundry room, community center, or ice rink. Where I once entertained friends in our backyard in Wesley Heights, I now see them on C-Span, PBS, and the nightly news. I watch as U.N. Ambassador Bill Richardson negotiates with world leaders and returned from Baghdad with the release of American prisoners; and I remember the drama of the White House ceremony when I saw the return of the Iranian hostages from a front row seat. Sometimes I am nostalgic for the proximity to the weighty events of the day. I will always enjoy the memory of entertaining Helen Thomas in our home, of having our neighbors, David and Susan Brinkley, pet-sit for our dog while I traveled to Athens on business. But invitations to the White House, to Senate and Embassy receptions, to seats in the Presidential Box at the Kennedy Center, all pale in comparison to the gratification I have found as a mother.

While a legislative assistant in the Senate, I remember hearing my colleagues comment condescendingly about the mothers playing with their children in Turtle Park, adjacent to the Japanese Embassy, rather than returning to the workplace. Since I was not married at the time, the choice of staying at home to raise a child did not even present itself and I did not feel offended, until years later when I heard echoes of the refrain about my own choice to stay at home with Niki. The very basic instinct to want to care for and nurture my child was called into question by a culture of ambition and achievement that put a premium on professional success, rather than the more inchoate and subtle nuances of raising a child. These pressures were reinforced by the ambivalence of losing my recognized status in the workplace, of losing financial independence, and the frequent feeling of isolation and boredom that confront many new mothers. I was being marginalized in a place where I once was very comfortable—close to the center of power.

It was not an easy transition. I did not have the nannies and housekeepers to ease the burden, and the five loads of laundry waiting for me at the end of the day were sometimes daunting. My lunches at the

Maison Blanche were replaced by peanut butter sandwiches and the dinners at the Harrimans soon were taken over by the parent-teacher conferences and Brownie meetings. But love, molding and sustaining the bond with my daughter was far more compelling and substantial than the political and social events I used to attend. The overwhelming delight that I took with every expression of fondness and solicitude was so strong that the caresses and tender words with smiles far outweighed any public accomplishment that I had achieved. I was very proud when I was invited to attend a White House ceremony honoring individuals who had worked on human rights issues during the Carter presidency and I felt an inherent satisfaction that my work on behalf of Cypriot refugees was recognized. But again, my gift of motherhood was so infused with a spiritual quality that was extraordinary, that I could not think of any emotion more ardent in its intensity.

I was finally dealing in the real world of sleep deprivation, projectile vomiting, and "itsy-bitsy spider" rhymes. I joined with other mothers at story time at the local library, I shared my maternal concerns at the drop-in centers with other very talented mothers, and I began to help validate their choice to stay at home to raise their children. The women I met were quite accomplished in their fields, with MBA's from Harvard, Stanford, and Kellogg, and careers in banking, finance, law, and television production. We helped each other in our child-rearing roles and in our knowledge that we were providing the essential kindness and moral values that would hopefully be transmitted to our children over the long term. I had very little ambivalence and guilt in leaving my career, but I saw other women struggle with their decision even though they were aware that the nuances of the care and love they provided were so important. There was little societal support and respect for their decision. Their former colleagues and friends would be mythologized in articles of professional success, while their simple sacrifices and rather mundane contributions were trivialized in comparison.

I found the smaller necessary duties of motherhood to be far more satisfying than the legal briefs, Senate memoranda, or PR stratagems I used to prepare. I was dealing with the fresh originality and spontaneity of a toddler. The attachment and love has grown and the social and emotional experiences have amplified, and I have never lost sight of the depth and spiritual quality that motherhood has given to me. I see the brilliant demonstration of my efforts every time Niki expresses her concern for a friend, or mediates a dispute, or composes a poem for her grandparents or teacher. Her own strength, wisdom, and compassion is quite moving and she has dealt with loss and transition in a remarkable way. I have been infinitely more challenged and rewarded in teaching Niki what it takes to get along in this world than in amendments to the Foreign Assistance Act. I am able to formulate my own strategems for showing my daughter how to act in a wise and compassionate manner. I want to be the primary transmitter of values to my daughter, reinforced by her wonderful school and community. In the process, I have learned the most basic lessons of modesty and decency from other mothers who provide a support network to each other and have taken the time from their careers to pass on the things that can make a difference.

The budget debates, health care reforms, and conflicts in the Gulf can be dealt with by a myriad of talented lawyers, analysts, and diplomats, but only I can be Niki's mother for the most important years of her life. I have been far more gratified than I dared to expect and the complexity of the mother-child relationship is truly a gift that approaches the sacred. At the end of the day, I have no ambivalence about my choice, but there are professional and financial repercussions which are significant.

Although I have been emotionally satisfied with my decision, there is a very real price to be paid in the marketplace. When time for re-entry approaches, the commitment to raising a child is most seriously challenged, as gaps in a resume are looked at critically, and questions of ability are raised. I have been asked what I have done recently and my distance from the workplace has been raised as a significant obstacle to re-entering a work environment. Even though the years in and out of the workplace put women in touch with real life and humanize them, they are seen as a diversion from a linear career track. We are caught in a stereotypical bind of careerist or nurturing mom, when, in fact, one can complement the other. We try to construct work around values of balance, inclusion, and meaning in our lives. Mothers can comprehend constant demands, unquestioned commitment to goals, and gratifying rewards in the workplace, as well as at home. We need to acknowledge and accommodate our real lives and demands as women as we try to provide for our families, both in emotional and financial content. We need to enter into a conversation where the values of community and home are important in both worlds and should not be stifled or hidden. We need to be present in the fleeting moment that is our children's lives and also be able to provide for them and ourselves in a work environment that is supportive. And we need help along the way.

Chapter 2

ꕥ

Home-Schooling in the 1990s

KATHERINE A. KERSTEN*

I have four children, ages eight to thirteen, and I quit work as an attorney 12 years ago when my second child was born, because as they say, I just "couldn't do it all." For 12 years, I have been doing a fair amount of writing and public policy work, but I have always managed to find a way to work this into my family's schedule.

I have been fortunate, of course, to have a husband who encourages and supports me and the children in every possible sense, and has made our way of life possible. I would like to talk about the role of the family in education, and how I have come to see myself in my role as a parent, as my children's first and most important teacher. Most particularly, I would like to talk about how I have become something I never thought I would become—a home-schooler. I would like to tell you a little bit about what this adventure has been like for my daughter, Julia, and me.

---

*Katherine A. Kersten is president of the Center for the American Experiment. She is an attorney and a writer.

Since college, I had always been interested in education—in what subjects should be taught and how they can best be taught. But when I became a parent, my idea of what education is—my vision of education—changed and expanded, and here's how that happened.

When my children were small, I attended, for a number of years, early childhood education classes, which I am sure some of you have participated in. There are lots of mothers there, and you sit around in a room, and you talk about toilet training and discipline and other pressing issues with a "facilitator." Well, everywhere in these classes, the leader would always raise the same question: "What do you want most out of life for your son or daughter?" The women in my group were always good and devoted mothers. What struck me though, watching them encounter this question, is that they seemed to be disconcerted by it. They seemed to be slightly embarrassed, and they would hesitate for a moment, and then they would say, "I just want her to be happy." And everyone would nod, that's right.

I could tell that most of these mothers wanted more for their children than a personal sense of well-being, but they did not seem to know quite how to articulate it. So having gone to Notre Dame in a "Great Books" program, when my turn came, I always said something like this: "I want her to be wise, and just, and good, and courageous, and honest, and self-reliant, and a productive member of society. I want her to fulfill her responsibilities as a citizen." And these mothers would listen and say, "Yes, that's right, that's what I want, too."

As I encountered this moral vacuum, it occurred to me that in our society today, there are many good people who want to do the right thing, but who are beginning to lose the language and the categories of thought that make this possible. As a result, I began to think more about my obligations as a parent—not just my obligation to help my children to be happy or to "be themselves," but my obligation to help them be a very specific kind of human being. It seemed to me, as I thought about it, that true education is about more than the acquisition of knowledge and skills. True education is about the molding of character, the molding of the whole man or woman in accordance with an ideal. This concept was first formulated by the ancient Greeks—the first great educators—and they called it "paidea," the process of shaping the quintessentially Greek character. Of course, "paidea" has strongly influenced the traditional notion of liberal education which means the education of a free man or woman, and was the animating wisdom behind American education of the 19th century. Unfortunately, we've largely lost that tradition today.

Well, three years ago I actually had the chance to put into practice my developing ideas about education. I had the chance to do it at my own kitchen table, where I found myself teaching my 10 year old daughter—who is now 12.

My home-schooling adventure started this way. My daughter, who was then in fourth grade, is dyslexic and has struggled with education from her kindergarten days. Now, I knew that school was tough for her, but I really was not prepared, going in for her end of year conference, for what her teacher had to tell me—"Julia is regressing." Her teacher said that she was staring out the window and she was not engaged in class, and I thought, "oh gosh, what am I going to do?" We had her in four schools and then it came down to me. I was the bottom line, and it had to be me who pulled her out of the situation.

I started by seeking out a fledgling home school support group that one of my friends had told me about. As I walked into this group's meeting for the first time, I felt very wary. I thought, "Who are these people? What will they look like?" I was prepared for the worst. But it was with great relief that I discovered my fellow home-schoolers looked a whole lot like me. Around the table I saw women from a variety of interesting backgrounds. There was a biology major who wanted to help our girls dissect a fetal pig. There was a mother whose living room was lined with brightly illustrated Latin exercises. There were mothers of 10 and 12 year old children who were studying at the University of Minnesota.

Most of these women were self-starters. They were independent, resourceful, hardworking women who wanted something that they could not find anywhere for their children, and were willing to sacrifice to build it themselves. As I came to know them, they really restored my faith in this nation—in the power of people without government, to take responsibility for their own well-being and the well-being of their families, and to do great things as a result.

That was two years ago. Our group is going strong and I will give you an idea of some of the things that we have done. We have a newsletter that our children write, design, illustrate, and publish themselves with their own compositions and poetry. We have group classes every two weeks. We all meet for lunch and we have classes taught by professional teachers—Spanish class, Latin class, public speaking, folk dancing class, and an art class. We have field trips of all kinds: concerts, plays, and trips to the airport to see its inner workings. We have service projects, an adopt-a-grandparent program at the local nursing home, and visits to homeless shelters. We have home-school gymnastic classes, and other sports opportunities.

My favorite activity is our American Girls' History Club. Some of you may be familiar with the American Girl dolls—six dolls that are linked to various periods in American history. For interested girls, we have six parties a year, each taking a particular period as its theme. For example, when we had a party for Kirsten, the Swedish immigrant girl, we all dressed in Scandinavian costumes and we had a wonderful banquet of ludefisk and fruit soup. We did Swedish weaving on a loom, painted wooden spoons, and learned Scandinavian folk dances. A wonderful time was had by all.

In addition, we have speakers for parents, curricula fairs, holiday parties, and graduation ceremonies. People think of socialization as a problem for home-schooled children. I think for most, it is not a problem at all. My daughter has the closest friends she has ever had who also happen to be the nicest friends she has ever had. But the best part of home-schooling for us has been the educational odyssey that has taken place at our kitchen table. I have seen these years as an opportunity to introduce my daughter to the best that has been thought and said. I try to get her to begin to think about what the good life is for human beings, and to ask questions about what is good, true, and beautiful. I have not used a set curriculum, particularly so I could use remedial materials that would assist her in reading decoding, and other things that most kids her age would not need. But I have relied heavily on E.D. Hirsch, on his wonder "cultural literacy" books, and on a magnificent book called "Designing Your Own Classical Curriculum," by Laura Berquist. I have used lots of out-of-print history books from before 1960 days—they always seem to be the best ones. We have become fixtures at our local library, and have found the resources available through home-schooling catalogs to be absolutely extraordinary. We have found that the sky is the limit in home-schooling. We start our day in the car, taking my other children to their schools. During that time, Julia memorizes poetry: selections from Shakespeare, Colleridge—the "Rhyme of the Ancient Mariner" and "Kubla Khan"—William Blake, Emily Dickenson, James Whitcomb Riley. When she finishes a poem she recites it to her father, and then writes it down and illustrates it. We put the finished product into the poetry notebook, so she has a record of all of her work. I think that her mind has been furnished with the best that English literature has to offer, as a result of 15 minutes a day in the car.

History has become Julia's favorite subject. In fifth grade, for American history, we used Joy Hakim's outstanding 10-volume series called "The History of US." It is very detailed, vivid, and stimulating. We supplemented "The History of US" with historical novels about Thomas Jefferson, Ben Franklin, and other important figures. We have read poems like Emerson's "Concord Hymn," and Longfellow's "Paul Revere's Ride." I've read things to her that she could not read herself, like "The Courtship of Miles Standish," "Evangeline," and Patrick Henry's "Give Me Liberty or Give Me Death" speech, The Declaration of Independence, and Washington's Second Inaugural Address. Throughout this process, she wrote compositions. For example, I had her do essays on subjects like "If I lived in Colonial Williamsburg," which required her to draw together lots of the material we were reading and organize it in her own words.

In sixth grade, Julia and I did ancient history. We used a marvelous nine-volume set from the 1950s called "A Picturesque Story of History." When we did Greece, for example, we studied the philosophers—Socrates, Plato, Aristotle, the Stoics, and the Epicureans. We studied the origins of comedy and tragedy, and Julia made pictures of all the great Greek playwrights—Aeschylus, Socrates, Euripides, and Aristophanes. We watched some Greek plays, like a marvelous performance of "Iphigenia in Aulas." We also got a tape from the library of the "Iliad" chanted in ancient Greek and read a children's version of "The Odyssey." When we studied Mesopotamia, we found a children's version of the "Epic of Gilgamesh," and also read some adult books about the decoding the Rosetta stone.

When we did Rome, we watched Shakespeare's "Julius Caesar" and analyzed the speeches of Mark Antony and Brutus. We read portions of Marcus Aurelius' "Meditation" and the Roman poets. At the end of our study, we went to the Art Institute and spent an afternoon looking at Egyptian, Assyrian, Greek, and Roman art.

With all this work, Julia's scores on her standardized tests improved significantly, although the dyslexia is certainly still a challenge. Nationally, in fact, home-schooled children do very well on standardized tests. In Minnesota, on the Iowa Basic Skills tests, they perform in the 83rd percentile.

There are about a million children being home-schooled today in this country and, for most of us, home-schooling has been a very rewarding adventure. When I look around at these group meetings, I see confirmation of the Founding Fathers' belief that ordinary people are capable of governing themselves—of discerning what is best for them. The Founders believed that American citizens have the right to pursue happiness and the good life in the way that seems best to them. It seems to me that all of us, whether we choose to educate our children at home or not, should give thanks that we have the freedom to do so.

Chapter 3

Counter-Cultural Womanhood or Why I Am Not a Feminist

Jennifer Roback Morse*

At this time two years ago, I appeared to be the quintessential modern woman. I had my doctorate in economics. I had a tenured position at a well-known research center in a large state university. I had a husband and two small children. We had a nice house in the Virginia suburbs of Washington, D.C. Because of the flexibility of university life, I was able to meet my professional responsibilities and still take good care of my kids. I seemed to "have it all."

Many women withdraw from the labor force after the arrival of children, and my children were certainly a factor in my decision. But my relationship with my husband proved to be the decisive factor that led to reordering my priorities. Because of the priority of my marriage relationship, I can no longer bear to call myself a feminist of any sort,

---

*Jennifer Roback Morse is an economist. She has taught at Yale University and George Mason University. She is currently at the Hoover Institute in California at Stanford University.

not an individualist feminist, not a libertarian feminist, and not an equity feminist. Let me explain what I mean.

The modern feminist movement consists of two strands—an economic and political strand on one hand, and a social and cultural strand on the other hand. The feminist approach to politics and economics has been statist and collectivist, while the feminist approach to social and cultural issues has been libertarian and individualistic. Some women who are skeptical of the economic and political aspects of feminism might be attracted to the seemingly libertarian aspects of the feminist approach to personal issues. But I have come to the conclusion that the modern feminist movement has been as mistaken in the social area as in the economic area. I can no longer call myself a feminist of any stripe. No modifying adjective will suffice to wipe away the vast destruction wrought under the banner of feminism.

You will see for yourself how the approach I have arrived at differs from feminism as it has most often understood itself. My approach is individualistic in the sense that an individual woman can make a huge difference in the quality of her own life and the lives of those around her. We do not need to wait for vast shifts in public opinion, huge commitments of government resources or even big changes in the attitudes of our family members. Now, back to my own story.

One aspect of feminism that I always found appealing was the idea that married women should not be mere appendages of their husbands. I took the unexceptional statement that wives are not doormats to mean that I had the right, and possibly the duty, to "stand up for myself" inside the marriage. I had come to believe that my dignity as a modern woman depended upon prevailing in disagreements that would arise between my husband and myself.

You will probably not be surprised when I tell you that we quarreled often and bitterly. I frequently asked myself the questions that any self-respecting modern career woman would ask. Is this really the right man for me? Is he really pulling his weight in this household? Are my needs being met in this relationship? Can I make it on my own? Would the children and I be better off without him?

In the aftermath of one such episode, I went to confession one Saturday afternoon. I forget what sin of mine I had twisted into an excuse to complain about my husband's behavior. But I shall never forget what the priest said to me: "Almighty God has put this man in the center of your life." Uh, oh. God is involved in this. Father Bradley had never led me astray before. Suppose he is right about this? That was my first counter-cultural question. Why would God put this particular man in the center of my life? On another occasion, I was complaining to a friend of mine. I told her that I would like to quit my job and stay home with the children full-time, but I was afraid that I might end up on my own. I concluded that my marriage was held together with fear. She replied, "Yes, and it could have been held together with love." Uh, oh. Counter-cultural question number two: what would it be like to be in a marriage that was based more upon love than fear?

The combination of those questions was like a key turning the tumblers in a lock. What did I think love was anyhow? I knew that I wanted my husband to accept me as I am, to give me emotional support and encouragement. I wanted him to accept any criticism from me about his faults and failings. At the same time, I demanded that he be completely tolerant of any shortcomings of mine. (In my parlance, he had character flaws; I just had shortcomings.)

It finally crossed my mind that he might want some of the same things from me that I wanted from him. He might want some forbearance and tolerance from me, rather than criticism. He might want some appreciation, rather than nagging.

I was measuring the relationship by what he did for me. I wanted his help, on my terms of course. I was sure that I knew the best way to raise kids and to discipline them. But my husband didn't want to be an assistant mom; he wanted to be a father. I was viewing love as a commodity that might or might not satisfy my needs. I had overlooked the fact that love might require something of me. I wanted him to make my well-being his highest priority, but I was unwilling to do the same for him. I was using my husband.

After a few of these counter-cultural reflections, it finally occurred to me that in spite of all my sophisticated education, I really knew almost nothing about love. Then it occurred to me just why God might put another person in the center of my life: for me to learn about love. I said to myself, "suppose Father Bradley is right. Let me put aside the question of whether or not to stay married. (The continual posing of that question was disruptive and destabilizing to the marriage.) Let me assume instead that God really has put this man at the center of my life for my own good." Counter-cultural question number 3: what can I do, independently of anything my husband might do, to improve this relationship? I made a decision to take the initiative. Instead of continually demanding that he shape up, I could go first.

Since I really knew so little about love, it was hard to know where to begin. The only thing I did know was to ask for help. So I made this a part of my prayer life. "Lord, I don't know squat about love. Please teach me how to love this man." This is the kind of prayer that is only answered slowly and in dribs and drabs. But there is one incident that stands out in my memory.

I can recall saying to myself in a fit of righteous indignation, "This man is totally incapable of accepting the slightest bit of negative information about himself. He can't stand criticism, or even mild suggestions that he should change." Well, I certainly enjoyed that moment of feeling superior to him. In fact, I had enjoyed many such moments over the years. The thought came to me. "So, accept it as a fact that he can't stand criticism, at least not from you. Have you ever gotten anything you wanted from getting in his face? Be reasonable; what you are doing is not working. Stop doing it."

I made a decision to stop criticizing my husband. It was relatively easy at first to keep my mouth shut and not criticize him out loud. But as I started keeping track of this behavior, I came to realize just how much I indulged in criticizing him in my mind. That habit of the mind was much harder to root out than the habit of the mouth.

Around the same time, I made a decision to stop quarreling with my husband, and to stop complaining. It was amazing how quiet the relationship became once I stopped criticizing, quarreling, and complaining. Now you know that I have certainly given up any claim to be a feminist!

About a year later, my husband got a phone call. We had originally moved to the Washington area for me to take a university job. He had grown increasingly dissatisfied with his job, and convinced that there was nothing in the vicinity of the Beltway for a nuts and bolts engineer. He had put his resume on the Internet. He got a call from a high tech firm in Silicon Valley offering him an opportunity for a much better job.

All that time, I had been asking God to teach me how to love. When my husband told me about the job offer, I astonished myself. I said to my husband, "if you think this is the right job for you and that this move is the right thing for the whole family, then I will go with you and we will make it work." I was amazed at how easy it was for me to say that and mean it. It was, as the kids say, "a no-brainer." My friends started telling me I was a counter-cultural radical.

Without abdicating my own responsibility in the slightest, I must say that even the tiny corner of the feminist mindset that I had accepted was a contributing factor in my self-righteousness. Feminist ideology offers a justification for quarreling over a large set of issues. I had accepted that piece of the feminist world view, because it was fun to see myself as superior to my husband. I enjoyed winning and feeling self-righteous about it.

Now, I ask myself, "is having my own way on this issue worth the price of the harmony of our household?" Very few issues are worth that price. Contrary to my fears, I found that my self-esteem can survive the experience of not having my own way. I can say, "this issue seems to be important to him. Can I give him this?" Usually the answer is, "sure, why not?"

Perhaps some of you think that I have overreacted to feminism when I say that I now defer to my husband when I can reasonably do so. Perhaps I have. I have some particular personality traits that made me vulnerable to this aspect of feminism. I am aggressive, high-strung, easily upset, and bossy. Perhaps I embraced this part of the feminist agenda more eagerly than most of you, and therefore caused myself more harm. Perhaps the seemingly extreme measures I have taken will not seem appropriate for each of you. I am sure many of you would never have considered giving yourself permission to quarrel with your husband the way I did. And for you, this whole discussion is probably a big yawn. I hope you can bear with me, while I say a few more words to those in the audience who might be wondering how a modern woman can start sounding like something out of the dreaded fifties.

When my husband and I have different ideas about how to do something, we used to get into a power struggle. But now my policy is to decide in advance that I will defer to his decisions whenever I can reasonably do so. I tell him what I want and why, and then see what happens. I found out something truly amazing: I actually end up getting more of what is best for me by not arguing. Here is why.

In the midst of a quarrel, people often end up defending the weakest possible case for their position. This is because your opponent picks out your weakest point and attacks it. (Notice that in a quarrel, he is no longer "husband", or "friend," but "opponent.") In the heat of battle, one is seldom rational enough to say, "oh yes, you are so right. How silly of me to not see that." We are much more likely to dig in our heels and attempt to defend ourselves, even our bad ideas done for not very good reasons. The idea that a woman should "stand up for herself" inside the marriage assumes that all her preferences, ideas, and inclinations are equally worthy and that her well-being depends on all those preferences being satisfied. As a matter of fact, most people have a lot of trouble having a reasonable perspective on their own wishes. One of the greatest gifts that a friend can give is exactly that: perspective.

He assigns my preferences a much higher weight in his decisions now that I am not in a power struggle with him. It is far easier for him to be generous with me, when I am not in his face making categorical demands. We can have a reasonable conversation and, most often, we both end up modifying our positions to some extent. We actually learn something from each other.

Although no one can really control another person, we can make it easier for certain qualities present in a person to emerge. If I present a demand to my husband, that action of mine will most likely call forth defensiveness and counter-demands from him.

On the other hand, I can make it easier for his love and care for the family to emerge by trusting him. He has learned to believe that I trust him to consider the good of the whole family, and not just his preferences and convenience. Many times, I have seen him stand up taller, pull his shoulders back further and do the right thing. I know in my heart that trusting him, by being willing to follow his lead, brings out the best in him.

Let me give an example: home schooling. When we moved to California, we were appalled by the poor quality of the schools we encountered. My inclination was to keep the children home and educate them at home. My husband wanted to try and find more satisfactory school arrangements than the ones we first found. I did my best to do as he asked. We found better schools. I wanted to keep the kids home and keep the family together. Against the good of family unity and better schooling, my husband saw another good: the good of the family members (me included) being able to confront the larger world outside the family and to perform in that world.

Because we resolved the issue without quarreling, we have given our family the best chance for being successful at the path we have taken. We can modify our approach as the situation develops. Neither of us has our egos attached to getting the particular outcome we want. We both want what is best for the whole family. If Plan A doesn't work as expected, neither of us is so attached to it that we have to defend it heart and soul. We can talk about it and move on to Plan B, or Plan C, or some new plan neither of us has yet conceived of.

The demand that "the woman should have the same right to final decision-making authority" is a feminist demand. It is not necessarily the way most people, if untutored in feminist ideology, would frame the issue. I can tell you without hesitation that there has been tremendous power for me in surrendering the final decision-making authority to my husband.

What does "power" mean? Does having power in a relationship mean getting my own way all the time? Mercy, I hope not. That is the attitude of a two-year-old. I have to admit that having my own way is not necessarily the greatest good for me, or my family. I also have to admit that having my own way was often my highest priority.

If, alternatively, power means being able to have a happy life, in the company of my family, then who makes the decision is ultimately not the most important thing. The spirit in which the decision is made carries independent weight. There are often several perfectly acceptable outcomes to a decision. It is unnecessary for me to insist on my particular vision in order to arrive at a good enough result.

Second, giving up the power struggle is something I could do unilaterally. I cannot, by myself, insist that he surrender the final decision-making authority to me, as a rule, or even on a case-by-case basis. He might very well do so. In fact, he frequently does. There are numerous issues about which he absolutely accepts my judgement, no questions asked. The point is that I cannot demand that of him.

Finally, some of you may be wondering how often I prevail in these differences of opinion, as compared with how often he prevails. I honestly can not answer that question. I can tell you that our decisions are sometimes resolved by doing what I first proposed, rather than what he first proposed. I can honestly tell you that I am no longer keeping very close track of who wins how many arguments. As compared with two years ago, keeping score is simply a non-issue. And that is the greatest freedom of all. Releasing myself from the need to quarrel, and the need to win has freed up a tremendous amount of energy that can be used for other, much more pleasant activities.

When my husband read the first draft of this article, he thought it was misleading. He said, "You make it sound as if you follow me around, and we always do what I want. You still state your thoughts and feelings very clearly. You have just given up nagging me until you get your own way." The fact of the matter is that I had a pretty big character flaw, and I was hiding behind my image as "modern career woman" to avoid correcting it. It is still difficult for me to have a clear perspective on this issue.

I have a better life without those tattered remnants of feminist ideology layered over me. My life has changed in some obvious ways. I do not work full-time outside the home. We live in a tiny rented house in Silicon Valley. But even the parts of my life that appear to be the same have been transformed. Our little house is a home, and not a hotel into which we all collapse after spending the day at work or school. I am still married, but I do not quarrel with my husband. I am no longer trying to do a full-time job on a part-time schedule. I do contract work for various think tanks. My children still go to school each day. But we are no longer pushing the children away from us for our convenience. Rather, we are easing them out the door from time to time for their own good.

This is why I can no longer call myself a feminist. I figured out pretty quickly that feminist economics was ridiculous and feminist politics tyrannical. I knew that the feminist claim that all men threaten all women at all times was baloney. But I had accepted a little, seemingly harmless piece of the feminist world view. I picked out an idea that made me feel important, and that fed a major weakness in my character.

The deep flaw in feminism is that it has no place for love, for the mutual giving of one person to another that allows both to deepen and grow. Feminism is the last remnant of the Marxist worldview that sees every human relationship in terms of conflict and struggle. There is no place in either Marxism or feminism for cooperation or complementarity.

Can we have both love and a career? Perhaps so, but not if we make the career our top priority.

So what remains of feminism? For me, nothing. Am I a feminist in the sense of valuing women's expanding career opportunities and labor force participation? I value those things, but I am unwilling to give credit to the feminist movement for the opening of the labor market to women. For that trend was well under way long before Betty Friedan wrote *The Feminine Mystique*. The trend toward greater labor force participation of married women began at the turn of the century, and had a sharp explosion during WWII. While many women left the labor force after the war, the trend toward greater participation continued on the upward path that had started as early as 1900.

I owe nothing to the feminist movement for my doctorate in economics, a field of which most of them are entirely ignorant and of which few of them entirely approve. I owe a great deal to the people who did help me attain an education, my mother and father, my older brothers, my first husband, and the gentlemen at the University of Rochester who trained me. Our entry into the universities and the labor market could have taken place without all of the rancor and poisonous ideology that we have all had to suffer through.

When we founded the Women's Freedom Network five years ago, Rita and I and the others hoped we could become a platform for an alternative women's movement. We wanted to offer a opportunity to develop a women's movement that would be grounded in reality and not in fantasy. Our Network is a diverse group of women and men. The guiding principle that holds our group together is a respect for the truth. We are committed to collecting and presenting facts, even facts that have become unpopular. We are committed to telling the truth about what we have done, even when the truth might be embarrassing. It is in that spirit that I have offered these remarks tonight.

Chapter 4

ஐ

Joint Custody of Children

RONALD K. HENRY*

Let's begin with the basics. Children are born with two parents. Children want, love, and need two parents. Children are in the joint custody of both parents during the marriage.

During the marriage, we know that the status of the child is to have pure and unrestricted joint custody with unlimited access to both parents. The question for us is what should the law do when that marriage breaks apart? Who should have the burden of proof? The one who wants to continue the child's access to both parents or the one who wants to claim sole ownership of the child? Where should the burden of proof lie when there's going to be a change from the existing unrestricted access to both parents?

When you think about a custody order, bear in mind that it's a very simple legal concept. A custody order is just an injunction. We take people who previously had unrestricted freedom, people who previously

---

*Ronald K. Henry is an attorney in Washington, DC, who works as a public advocate on behalf of family and childrens issues.

had unrestricted access to their children, and now we enjoin them from exercising part of that freedom. Lawyers know the rule for dealing with injunctions in every other area of the law—*i.e.*, you impose the minimum necessary restriction on the parties' prior freedom. You put only the smallest imposition, the smallest restriction on them necessary to resolve the dispute at hand. This rule of minimum necessary restriction should also apply to injunctions involving child custody. You shouldn't go to a disruptive extreme like sole custody when a less restrictive solution is available.

If, as we all know, those children were in joint custody during the marriage, we ought to work very hard to preserve for the children, for their best interest, as much of that preexisting joint custody, as much of that access to both parents, as we can. When a divorce comes, does a child have less need or more need for the involvement of both parents? In my opinion, the child's need for both parents is actually greater because of the insecurity created by the divorce itself. If we care about children's best interests, we need to send a message through our laws that encourages the continued involvement of both parents, that encourages continued shared parenting, and that imposes only the minimum necessary restrictions just as we would do with any other kind of injunction.

Think about what a custody battle actually is. Two parents go into court and stand before a judge, each of them begging to spend more time with the child. What message do we want to send to people in this community? Have you heard one opponent of joint custody say that the children of this country are suffering from an excess of parenting or an excess of fathering or that children spend too much time with either of their parents? Of course not. We know that just the opposite is true.

We know that children are suffering from the absence of their parents. We know that our children are suffering from insufficient parenting. What is the message that we should be sending through our courts? If we care about the best interests of children, the message we should send is that we want to encourage the maximum continued involvement of both parents. Continue for them the joint custody that existed during the marriage, take away from those children as little as you absolutely must, and presume a continuation of two parents.

We have a saying in our community that "It takes a village to raise a child." By what theory of the child's best interests should a court come in and issue an order restricting one parent to mere visitor status? When you have two fit and loving parents, when you have two parents coming to the court and saying, "please give me more time with my child," shouldn't we throw up our hands and say, "Hallelujah," here is a child who is loved, here is a child who has two parents who want to be involved, let us see what we can do to maximize the contributions of both of these good people?

Instead, we have a very perverse system under which the judge says, "No, no, I'm sorry, my job is to pick a winner and pick a loser here." Well, when you pick a winner and pick a loser in a custody fight, all you've done is guarantee that the child is the loser because that child walked into court with two parents and walks out with only one. The winner-loser mentality that has driven child custody in the United States is antithetical to the best interests of the child. It doesn't matter what social pathology you look at—teenage pregnancies, drug abuse, suicide, low self-esteem, school dropout—you can go through the whole litany of pathologies that the government has to spend money to try to cure. Every single one of them is linked to family breakdown and parental absence. We don't have an excess of parenting. We have a shortage of parenting.

Let's put into place a law that says it is the policy of the courts to encourage the maximum involvement of both parents and to preserve for each child the joint custody in which that child was born and which continues by nature and by the law until a judge intervenes and takes it away. We don't need to take it away. We need to have a law that says you both are still Mom and Dad.

Look at the situations that have been in the newspapers recently, such as the *Prost v. Green* litigation.[1] I've talked with people on both sides of that case. You know what they both tell me? They both tell me they're scared. They're scared that they might lose custody, that they might be reduced to visitor status. So rather than run that risk, they each go in and fight like crazy. You've seen some of that in the newspapers. Each of them has said they would be willing to accept joint custody, but both remain fearful that if they go into court and acknowledge a willingness to accept joint custody, they will be deemed to have already given away half the loaf while they still run the risk of losing everything. These people run the risk of being reduced to a mere visitor to their own child, so they feel that they have to fight to be the one who emerges as the winner out of a desperate fear that otherwise they'll end up being the one who's the loser.

The purpose of joint custody is to get past winners and losers, to say to both litigants, "Relax, at the end of this you're both still going to be

Mom and Dad. You're both going to have substantial relationships with your children." Now, I really need to talk about some of the distortions and stereotypes and outright falsifications that occur when the opponents of joint custody produce their media sound bites.

Let's start with the claims that are made about cases where conflict exists between the parents. You keep hearing the notion of, "Oh, well, if the parents are in conflict, we can't possibly have joint custody." Of course conflict is bad for children. Conflict during a marriage is bad for children, conflict in sole custody is bad for children, conflict anywhere is bad for children. But none of the opponents of joint custody who argued about conflict ever asked you to compare directly the logic of the choices that are actually in front of you. We're not comparing joint custody against Ozzie and Harriet, we're comparing joint custody against sole custody.

Think for a moment which is more likely to engender hostility, or to create conflict—a situation in which both parents are told, "Relax, you're not going to lose your role as a parent," or a situation in which the court says, "I'm going to pick a winner and pick a loser. Choose your weapons and come out fighting, the last one left standing is the winner." Sole custody determinations are the source of the conflict. Legislation must be designed to reduce that conflict, reduce fear, and work for the best interests of the children. Ask the opponents of joint custody which is more likely to create conflict—a winner/loser dichotomy or sharing. That's an easy choice.

A related claim made by these opponents is that joint custody forces unwilling parents to interact with each other. Again, they are comparing joint custody to Ozzie and Harriet, they are not comparing it to sole custody. Remember that parents have to interact with each other in a sole custody situation. In sole custody, however, they interact from a basis of hostility. They interact from a basis of power and powerlessness. They interact from a basis in which one parent has been declared to be the loser and that parent is ever fearful of losing still more, of losing every last shred of contact and is ever struggling to try to get back into the child's life and restore what was taken away by a piece of paper, a judicial decree. Shared parenting gets away from all those conflicts. Shared parenting says you're both still Mom and Dad. Neither of you has lost your child. Neither of you is the owner of the child with power to exclude the other. There is no doubt that the shared parenting approach is more healthy for children.

Let me turn now to the hostile parent "veto" power that's been proposed by some of the opponents of shared parenting. Can you think of any other area of law where the statute grants permission for one of the litigants to come in and veto a proposed remedy that was in the best interests of the parties and otherwise permitted by the law? Can you imagine, in any other setting, the audacity of this demand, the hubris of daring to come forward and say that the most hostile parent ought to have the power to veto the other parent's involvement, ought to have the power to veto the child's best interest in shared parenting? What theory of best interest could ever suggest that one parent can veto the child's best interest and reject shared parenting?

The opponents of joint custody acknowledge that 42 states have shared parenting in their statutes and the rest have it in common law. They can't cite to you a single one that allows this veto that they are urging you to adopt. They like to talk about California but that's one of their greatest falsehoods. California didn't retreat from shared parenting. California is in the forefront of shared parenting; 75 to 80 percent of all custody decrees in California include joint parenting and it's even higher in some other states. In Minnesota, for example, it's in excess of 90 percent. Shared parenting is here. The revolution has arrived and it's time for the remaining states to catch up.

California's status is particularly interesting because of the way that it has been distorted in the opponents' statements about joint custody. California was under siege a few years ago. Several groups that didn't like joint custody went to the California legislature with an agenda of approximately 30 separate amendments trying to gut the joint custody provisions in California's law. They utterly failed. What California did instead, was that it passed a very simple clarification of its statute which states that shared parenting is equally available as an alternative to sole custody. California has one of the clearest laws repudiating the notion that sole custody is preferred and that shared parenting is, somehow, an ugly stepchild.

California went two steps further, steps that none of the opponents of shared parenting ever want to talk about, and you'll be able to find this very easily in the California statute books. First, the statutes say right up front that it is the policy of the State of California to encourage the child's frequent and continuing contact with both parents. Second, the statute says that we like shared parenting, but we know that sometimes we may not be able to have equal time with both parents; perhaps distance doesn't allow it. In those cases where we have to give the majority of the residential time to one parent, we are going to give a preference to that parent who shows the greater willingness and ability to cooperate in keeping the other parent involved. It is on this point that the real fraud of some of the opponents becomes apparent. You have probably heard opponents saying that they don't like the cooperative parent provisions of some joint custody statutes. Can you imagine that? How dare they demand that we ought not to encourage cooperation, that we ought not to encourage demilitarization of divorce. You've heard every day of the horrors of divorce for children. Of course we should encourage cooperation. Of course we should teach both of the parents to get along with one another and to work for the child's best interest. Sole custody doesn't do that. Sole custody says that only one parent is going to be left standing at the end of the day. We need to get to the other side, we need to recognize what these kids are born with, want, love, and need two parents.

Another set of issues the opponents raise is about control. They say the parents asking for shared parenting are just trying to control the other parent. Well, think about the fraud, the illogic of that for a moment. If you are asking a question about who's trying to control whom and one parent comes to you and says, " Judge, I would like to have shared parenting, so my child can have two parents" and the other parent says, "I want sole custody, I want to own this child," who's trying to exercise power? Who's trying to exercise control? Who is it that wants to be the one who's dominant and who is the one that has the interest of the child at heart?

Turning to the question of abuse, you'll find it to be quite contrary to the stereotypes and myths that are often put forward by the gender warriors. In every state, the data show that anywhere from two-thirds to three-quarters of all child abuse is committed by mothers, not by fathers. Are the opponents of shared parenting saying that all these mothers should be disqualified from custody or do they want to be selective again and say that it is only fathers who should be disqualified? Let's be honest, let's be logical, let's look at this consistently.

Opposition to the submission of a parent's proposed parenting plan in custody cases is what I find to be the most despicable among the arguments raised by the opponents of shared parenting. I think there ought to be no room at all in this nation for racist, classist, elitist arguments that our citizens are too stupid to fill out a form that indicates their desires for the upbringing of their own children. There is nothing difficult about letting parents indicate for themselves how they would care for their children and providing that information to judges. There is nothing that requires this to be done by lawyers or by a judge.

We should be encouraging our parents to come forward and look at the tasks, look at the burdens of raising a child, and fill out that form. When they sit down and look at that form and they realize how big a job it is to properly care for a child, they will step back and think, "You know, this is a job that's kind of hard to take on all by myself. It's to my advantage, as well as to my child's advantage, to share this burden because two parents can do a better job." Child custody law should apply one of the very simplest propositions in mathematics—two is more than one. Two parents can do more than one. A single parent may do all that he or she can, but there's no doubt that the active involvement of a second committed parent adds a lot and makes it better for the child.

You have also heard noise about child support and how terribly that was going be impacted if we have shared parenting. One of the answers to this is a study by Professor Sanford Braver of Arizona State University, which is to my knowledge the only controlled study in the nation of what happens to child support when you have shared parenting. Professor Braver's conclusion was that, "We found that the groups differed significantly in terms of how much financial support was paid. When sole custody was the arrangement, despite the father's wishes, only 80 percent was paid; when joint custody was awarded, despite opposition by one of the parents, child support zoomed to almost perfect compliance, 97 percent compliance." If you care about child support, if you care about reducing welfare dependency, joint custody does it. Don't allow people to come to you and make policy by anecdote. Look at the research, and look at what you know as a matter of simple logic. An actively involved parent is more likely to provide financial support along with emotional and physical support than is a visitor.

The study by Professor Braver is the only empirical study I am aware of which has examined side by side sole custody settings and joint custody settings where the joint custody was imposed over the objection of one of the parties. Remember, the objection you have heard from opponents is that, while they admit joint custody works where it is agreed to, they argue that it can't work where it is imposed. This is the only study that has examined forced sole custody versus forced joint custody. Professor Sanford Braver has been working in this area for a good many years, principally under grants from the National Institutes for Health. In some of his other research, Professor Braver has found that there are three principal predictors of child support compliance: the fairness of the original order, the obligor's frequent access to the child, and the obligor's work stability. A lot of this gets lost in our stereotypes, in the name calling that goes back and forth. The research does exist to show us and give us some guidance on these policy issues. Parents support their children; slaves run away.

Finally, I'm going to close with the issue of gender bias, because this debate has gotten somewhat fragmented along gender lines. Well, that's not quite right. What you find is that the people in favor of shared parenting include both men and women, mothers, fathers, children, advocates, a broad range of people. Where you find a very limited opposition, where you find a very limited perspective is in the people who are opposed to shared parenting. They do come at it from a single perspective, from the winner-take-all mentality that says that one parent should own that child, that one parent should have power over that child.

When you look at all of the information that is available about shared parenting today, think about who has the interests of children at heart. Who is it that wants the children to have the benefit of two parents and who is it that wants to use the children as a lever of power in the battle of the sexes? This is not a gender issue but it is an issue for some people who want to have power. Look at what Karen DeCrow, the former president of the National Organization for Women, has to say about the benefits to everyone from ending the winner/loser power game:

> If there is a divorce in the family, I urge a presumption of joint custody of the children. Shared parenting is not only fair to men and children, it is the best option for women. After observing women's rights and responsibilities for more than a quarter of a century of feminist activism, I conclude that shared parenting is great for women, giving time and opportunity for female parents to pursue education, training, jobs, careers, profession and leisure. There is nothing scientific, logical or rational in excluding men or forever holding women and children as if in swaddling clothes in an eternally loving bondage. Most of us have acknowledged that women can do everything that men can do. It is time now for us to acknowledge that men can do everything women can do.[2]

Men can be parents. Look at what Supreme Court Justice Ruth Bader Ginsburg has to say about her view and her goal for the future, her desire to see men taking a greater role in child care and child custody.[3] Look at the position of the National Center for Women and Retirement Research, an organization of more than 100,000 members which has endorsed shared parenting.[4] This is not a gender issue but there is a special interest group, there is a limited opposition, there are people who want to have control over children. I respectfully suggest that you reject their arguments for control and, if you care about the best interests of children, give them two parents. Let them keep the two parents that they had during the marriage. Don't allow sole custody to take that away from them. Now let me talk to you about the non-marital situation because frankly, in my view, there is no difference in terms of the outcome or the proper legal status. Bear in mind that each child is born with two parents. That child is born with two legal parents. We have child support proceedings regardless of marital status. There is no distinction made between the legal obligations imposed upon a marital father and a non-marital father.

In fact, if you look at the Supreme Court cases, *Clark v. Jeter*,[5] for example, about seven years ago, the Supreme Court established in a unanimous ruling that it was unconstitutional to treat a non-marital child in a way that was inferior to a marital child. What the court said there dealt with a statute that had a shorter statute of limitations for commencing a child support action for non-marital children than the statute of limitations for marital children. I think the state allowed something like nine years for marital children and only three years for non-marital children. The Supreme Court said, "Time out. You can't do that. You can't discriminate against non-marital children. They have got every bit as much right to the involvement, the resources, the wherewithal of the father. They have got every bit as much right to those two parents that they were born with as a marital child."

So, I would submit to you that as a constitutional matter, we would be very hard pressed to discriminate against the non-marital child. I would go further and put it into pragmatic terms. Most of the children who are born into a non-marital situation are not the result of casual one-night stands. These are parents who have known one another a long time. They have got a relationship. They are frequently and perhaps in the majority of the cases actually living together. They are involved, both of them, with respect to the child. Why in the world would we have a law that presumes that one of the parents is uninvolved? I think that just the opposite should be presumed.

We should, as a matter of the law serving as a moral force, as a matter of the law encouraging the best in all of our citizens, start with the presumption that we do want, that we do expect, that we do believe both parents are going to be involved. Surely, that won't be the case in all situations but isn't that where we want to start out? Don't we want to believe, don't we want to encourage both parents' involvement, and don't we again get back to the problem of there being no excess of parenting in this country? We should encourage more parenting.

Notes

1. *Prost v. Geene*, 675 A. 2d 471 (D.C. App. 1996)
2. Karen DeCrow, *Syracuse New Times*, January 5, 1994
3. *New York Times*, January 7, 1994, page B11
4. Letter to District of Columbia City Council Judiciary Committee Chairman, James Nathanson dated April 19, 1994, from Christopher L. Hayes, Ph.D., Director, National Center for Women and Retirement Research
5. *Clark v. Jeter*, 486 U.S. 456, 108 S.C 1916, 100 L.Ed.2d 465 (1988)

Chapter 5

Men, Family, and Fatherhood

Wade F. Horn, Ph.D.*

Fatherhood today is the "best of times and the worst of times." On the one hand, there is evidence that increasing numbers of men want to be more involved in the daily upbringing of their children than their own fathers were with them. These are the men who are present at the birth of their children as "labor coaches," accompany their children on school trips, take their children to doctor appointments, and read to their children at night. These are also the men who are taking advantage of parental leave policies at the birth of a child, use the newly installed diaper changing tables in public restrooms, and buy such books as *The Dad Zone*, *Daddy Cool*, *The Father's Almanac*, and (I hope) the *Better Homes and Gardens New Father Book*, which I co-authored. This new fatherhood consciousness is also evident in the recent mass gatherings of

*Wade F. Horn is a child psychologist. He is a former Commissioner for Children, Youth, and Families at HSS. He is the head of the National Fatherhood Initiative.

the Million Man March and Promise Keepers, at which hundreds of thousands of men vowed to be better husbands and fathers.

Unfortunately, it is also the worst of times for fatherhood. In 1960, the total number of children in the United States living in father absent families was less than 10 million. Today, that number stands at over ***23 million.***[1] Nearly 4 out of every 10 children in America reside in a home in which their biological father does not live. And things are getting worse, not better. By some estimates, 60 percent of children born in the 1990s are likely to live in a home without their dad.[2] For the first time in our history, the average experience of childhood now includes a significant amount of time living absent one's own father. The population most devastated by the problem of father absence is the African-American community. Today, sixty-three percent of African-American children live in father absent homes.[3] The problem, however, is by no means restricted to the African-American community. Indeed, the total of father-absent families is larger—and the rate of father absence is growing the fastest—in the white community.[4] Currently, nearly 13 million white children reside in father-absent homes, compared to approximately 6.5 million African-American children.[5]

For one million children each year, the pathway to a fatherless family is divorce.[6] The divorce rate nearly tripled from 1960 to 1980, before leveling off and declining slightly in the 1980s.[7] Today, at least 50 percent of first marriages now end in divorce, compared to 16 percent in 1960. No other industrialized nation has a higher divorce rate.[8]

The second pathway to a fatherless home is out-of-wedlock births. In 1960, about five percent of all births were out-of-wedlock. That number increased to 10.7 percent in 1970, 18.4 percent in 1980, 28 percent in 1990, and a staggering 33 percent today.[9] In the United States, the number of children fathered out-of-wedlock each year (approximately 1.3 million annually) now surpasses the number of children whose parents divorce (approximately 1 million annually).[10]

No region of the country has been immune to the growing problem of fatherlessness. Between 1980 and 1990, non-marital birth rates increased in every state of the Union.[11] During this time period, ten states saw the rate of non-marital births increase by over 60 percent. Furthermore, births to unmarried teenagers increased by 44 percent between 1985 and 1992.[12] In fact, 76 percent of all births to teenagers nationwide are now out-of-wedlock. In 15 of our nation's largest cities, the teenage out-of-wedlock birth rate exceeds 90 percent.[13] Overall, the percent of families with children headed by a single parent currently stands at 29 percent, the vast majority of which are father-absent households.[14]

In addition to the physical absence of fathers from the home, it is also apparent that many physically present fathers are nonetheless psychologically absent from the lives of their children. Overall, parents today spend roughly 40 percent less time with their children than did parents a generation ago.[15] One study found that almost 20 percent of 6th through 12th graders had not had a good conversation lasting for at least 10 minutes with at least one of their parents in more than a month.[16] In regard to fathers, a 1992 Gallup poll found that 50 percent of all adults agreed that "fathers today spend less time with their children than their fathers did with them."[17]

The fact of increasing physical absence of fathers from the homes of their children would not be so disturbing if, in fact, physically absent fathers continued to stay involved in the lives of their children. Unfortunately, research has consistently found that fathers who do not live with their children, whether through divorce or out-of-wedlock fathering, tend over time to become disconnected from their children, both financially and psychologically. Forty percent of children in father-absent homes have not seen their father in at least a year. Of the remaining 60 percent, only one in five sleeps even one night per month in their father's home. Overall, only one in six sees their father an average of once or more per week.[18] More than half of all children who don't live with their fathers have never even been in their father's home.[19]

Unwed fathers are particularly unlikely to stay connected to their children over time. Whereas 57 percent of unwed fathers are visiting their child at least once per week during the first two years of their child's life, by the time their child reaches 7 1/2 years of age, that percentage drops to less than 25 percent.[20] Approximately 75 percent of men who are not living with their children at the time of their birth never subsequently live with them.[21] There is evidence indicating that it may be worse for a child to be secure in a relationship with their father during the early part of that child's life, only to have that man disappear by the time they're in first or second grade.[22]

Even when unwed fathers are cohabiting with the mother at the time of their child's birth, they are very unlikely to stay involved in their children's life over the long term. Although a quarter of non-marital births occur in cohabiting couples, only four out of ten cohabiting unwed fathers ever go on to marry the mother of their children, and those that do are more likely to eventually divorce than men who father children within marriage.[23] Remarriage or, in cases of an unwed father, marriage to someone other than the child's mother, makes it especially unlikely that a non-custodial father will remain in contact with his children.[24]

In contrast to the reality of disconnected, unwed dads, we are being bombarded by the mass media with a new heroic figure—the involved, committed, and responsible unwed father. In the 1980s, our culture popularized the mythic homeless person who had run up against hard times (through no fault of his or her own, of course), but who really had a Ph.D. in philosophy from Harvard. The purpose of this myth was to shield ourselves from the harsh realities of homelessness, where domestic violence, drug abuse, prostitution, and alcoholism are the real common denominators. So too is this new myth of the involved, responsible, committed-for-the-long-term, unwed dad avoiding the harsh realities of pre-marital sex and our cultural retreat from marriage as an ideal. Seduced into believing that marriage is "only a piece of paper" and that "safe sex" never results in babies, ever increasing numbers of children are being conceived outside of wedlock. And with disastrous results—for the baby, for the mom, and even for the dad.

This doesn't mean an unwed father can't be an involved dad. Some are. Nor does it suggest we should not try to get and keep unwed fathers involved with their children. We should. But the available evidence suggests that this is a very difficult task. It does no one any good—not the father, not the mother and not the child—to pretend otherwise.

The absence of fathers in the home has profound consequences for children. Almost 75 percent of American children living in single-parent families will experience poverty before they turn eleven-years-old, compared to only 20 percent of children in two-parent families.[25] Children who grow up without their fathers are also more likely to fail at school or to drop out,[26] experience behavioral or emotional problems requiring psychiatric treatment,[27] engage in early sexual activity,[28] and develop drug and alcohol problems.[29]

Children growing up with absent fathers are especially likely to experience violence. Violent criminals are overwhelmingly males who grew up without fathers, including up to 60 percent of rapists,[30] 75 percent of adolescents charged with murder,[31] and 70 percent of juveniles in state reform institutions.[32] Children who grow up without fathers are also three times more likely to commit suicide as adolescents[33] and to be victims of child abuse or neglect.[34]

In light of these data, noted developmental psychologist Urie Bronfenbrenner has concluded:

> Controlling for factors such as low income, children growing up in [father absent] households are at a greater risk for experiencing a variety of behavioral and educational problems, including extremes of hyperactivity and withdrawal; lack of attentiveness in the classroom; difficulty in deferring gratification; impaired academic achievement; school misbehavior; absenteeism; dropping out; involvement in socially alienated peer groups, and the so-called 'teenage syndrome' of behaviors that tend to hang together—smoking, drinking, early and frequent sexual experience, and in the more extreme cases, drugs, suicide, vandalism, violence, and criminal acts.[35]

I do not mean to imply that single mothers cannot raise their children well. Of course they can and many do. Nor do I mean to imply that fatherlessness is the sole cause of every social ill facing our nation's children. I recognize that all problems are multiply determined. But what these data do suggest is this: if we are ever to improve the well-being of children in America, *first* we will have to reconnect men to the ideal of good and responsible fatherhood and in so doing reverse this three decade long slide toward a fatherless America. The question is how?

Since the 1950's, attempts to deal with fatherlessness have been mostly about paternity establishment and child support enforcement. This is not, of course, without merit. Any man who fathers a child ought to be held financially responsible for that child. But as important as paternity establishment and child support enforcement may be, they are by themselves unlikely to substantially improve the well-being of children for several reasons.

First, paternity does not equal child support. Only one in four single women with children living below the poverty line receive any child support from the non-custodial father.[36] Some unwed fathers, especially in low-income communities, may lack the financial resources to provide economically for their children. For these men, establishing paternity and a child support order may not translate into economic support for the child.

Second, even if paternity establishment led to a child support award, the average level of child support (about $3,000 per year[37]) is unlikely to move large numbers of children out of poverty. Some may move out of poverty at the margins. But absent changes in family structure or workforce attachment, moving from poverty to near poverty is not associated with significant improvements in child outcomes.[38]

Third, an exclusive emphasis on child support enforcement may only drive these men further away from their children. As word circulates within low-income communities that cooperating with paternity establishment but failing to comply with child support orders may result in imprisonment or revocation of one's driver's license, many may simply choose to become less involved with their children. Thus, the unintended consequence of such policies is to decrease, not increase, the number of children growing up with fathers, proving once again that no good policy goes unpunished.

Finally, an over-focus on child support enforcement ignores the many non-economic contributions that fathers make to the well-being of their children. While the provision of economic support is certainly important, it is neither the only nor the most important role that fathers play. Indeed, emphasizing fatherhood in largely economic terms has helped to contribute to its demise. After all, if a father is little more than a paycheck to his children, he can easily be replaced by a welfare payment.

If we want fathers to be more than mere cash machines to their children, we will need a public policy that supports their work as nurturers, disciplinarians, mentors, moral instructors and skill coaches, and not just as economic providers. But if paternity establishment and child support enforcement is not the answer, what is?

First, our culture needs to send a more compelling message to men as to the critical role they play in the lives of their children. Currently, fathers are generally seen as "nice to have around" and as a source of economic support, but are not understood as contributing much that is particularly unique or irreplaceable to the well-being of their children. Take, for example, the current focus on "deadbeat dads." Here, the focus is almost exclusively on the importance of absent fathers paying child support, with little attention given to the need for them to stay involved with their children psychologically.

One way to counter this rather limited view of the importance of fathers, is the use of public education campaigns. Recently, the National Fatherhood Initiative assisted the Virginia Department of Health in implementing a state-wide public education campaign emphasizing the unique and irreplaceable contributions of fathers to the well-being of their children and the importance of fathers spending time with their kids. The effectiveness of the campaign was evaluated by an independent team of researchers at the University of Virginia. The results indicated that one out of every three Virginians could recall seeing or hearing about the campaign, and that there were measurable shifts in the percentage of Virginians who believed that fatherlessness was the most consequential problem facing the Commonwealth. But public awareness and shifts in attitudes were not the only consequences of the campaign. In addition, these researchers found that 40,000 fathers reported spending more time with their children as a consequence of the campaign, and 100,000 non-fathers reported talking to a father and offering support and encouragement.[39]

Second, we need to reestablish the expectation that men should father children only in the context of committed and legal marriages. Americans love to get married. Over 90 percent of Americans will marry some time during their lifetime. The trouble is that Americans don't love to stay married. Estimates of the chances of a first marriage ending in divorce range from 50 to 67 percent, and the chance that a second marriage will end in divorce is about 10 percent higher than that for first marriages.[40]

Making matters worse, nearly one in four unmarried adults of prime marrying age is currently cohabiting with another adult. With so many persons cohabiting, it is little wonder that nearly 1 of every 3 children today are born out-of-wedlock.

Given that cohabitation is a very weak substitute for marriage, both government and the broader culture need to provide greater incentives and support for marriage. Government can help by eliminating systemic preferences that provide punishments for marriage and give advantages to single parent families over two-parent, married families. For starters, the federal government ought to revise the Earned Income Tax Credit (EITC) so that it no longer provides a marriage penalty for low-income workers with children who choose to marry. In addition, states should take advantage of the opportunity afforded them through welfare reform to provide explicit preferences for marriage by, for example, sending low-income married couples to the front of the line when distributing limited supply benefits such as slots in Head Start and public housing.[41] States should also follow the lead of Louisiana and pass covenant marriage legislation under which couples are offered the opportunity to *choose* a higher form of mutual commitment than that afforded under current no-fault divorce laws.

The private sector can help restore a marriage culture by encouraging the development of "community marriage policies." Spearheaded by Mike McManus, President of Marriage Savers, Inc., community marriage policies involve bringing together both public and private sector leaders, especially in the faith community, to resolve to provide more meaningful premarital counseling, including the use of premarital inventories assessing the couples long-term compatibility, as well as marital enrichment programs and divorce interventions. Community Marriage Policies have been credited with helping to reduce divorce rates by 19 percent over the past four years in Peoria, Illinois, and by 40 percent in Modesto, California, over the past ten years.

Third, all of our most important mediating structures of our society—churches, synagogues, schools, and civic organizations—should sponsor outreach and skill building programs for fathers, and especially new fathers. One of the most effective programs for reaching out to young, unwed fathers is run by the National Center for Responsible Fathering and Child Development in Cleveland, Ohio. The strength of this program is that it focuses on enhancing father-child emotional ties prior to seeking paternity establishment and child support. Experience from this program suggests that as the father increases his attachment to the child, his desire to claim the child as his own and to take care of his child also increases, including an increased desire to provide economic support. This is especially important given recent research suggesting that voluntary, informal child support payments may be even more beneficial to the well-being of children than court-ordered and enforced child support.[42]

Finally, while working to support marriage and fathers, we must also take seriously our obligation to reach out to the fatherless child. It is tragic that so many children are growing up without fathers. Indeed, there are communities in America today in which 90 to 95 percent of the children don't have a father in a home. How do we expect fatherless boys, growing up in fatherless communities, will come to understand what it means to be a decent husband and a good father? Where are they going to look for their models for fatherhood? To television? Do we really want Al Bundy from TV's *Married . . . With Children* serving as their role model for fatherhood? And without loving husbands and fathers in the home, how is it that daughters will grow up knowing what to expect and demand from future boyfriends and marital partners?

Clearly, providing positive adult male role models through mentoring programs must be a high priority. But in doing so, we must be neither naive nor superficial. Fatherless kids do not need another man to come into their lives for six or seven months and then leave. In reaching out to a fatherless child, adult mentors must understand the necessity of staying committed to that child throughout his or her childhood and even into adulthood. Otherwise, in the name of doing good, we will only succeed in further reinforcing the idea that men are untrustworthy and relationships extremely fragile.

For fatherhood, it is both the best of times and the worst of times. Increasing numbers of men are dissatisfied with the narrow role of breadwinning when it comes to being a father. And our society seems to be gaining a better understanding of the importance of fathers to the well-being of children and our nation. But we must not delude ourselves into believing that this means the struggle to renew fatherhood has been won. Indeed, with four out of ten children living absent their fathers, it is clear that the most important battles are in front of us. Achieving attitudinal change may be hard but behavioral change is even harder. And that is what our children need most of all.

Notes

1. Wade F. Horn, *Father Facts, Third Edition*. Gaithersburg, MD: The National Fatherhood Initiative, 1998.
2. Frank F. Furstenberg, Jr., and Andrew J. Cherlin, *Divided Families: What Happens to Children When Parents Part*. Cambridge, MA: Harvard University Press, 1991.
3. U.S. Bureau of the Census, *Statistical Abstract of the United States 1997*, U.S. Government Printing Office, Washington, D.C., 1997.
4. Wade F. Horn, *Father Facts, Third Edition*. Gaithersburg, MD: The National Fatherhood Initiative, 1998.
5. U.S. Bureau of the Census, *Statistical Abstracts of the United States 1997*, U.S. Government Printing Office, Washington, D.C., 1997.
6. Ibid.
7. U.S. Department of Commerce, Bureau of the Census, "Statistical Abstract of the United States, 1993," (Washington, D.C.: Government Printing Office, 1993).
8. National Commission on Children, "Just the Facts: A Summary of Recent Information on America's Children and Their Families," (Washington, D.C.: U.S. Government Printing Office, 1993).
9. Harry M. Rosenberg, Stephanie J. Ventura, Jeffrey D. Maurer, Robert L. Heuser, and Mary Freedman, *Births and Deaths in the United States, 1995*, Monthly Vital Statistics Report, 45, 1996.
10. Wade F. Horn, *Father Facts, Third Edition*. Gaithersburg, MD: The National Fatherhood Initiative, 1998.
11. Stephanie J. Ventura, Christine A. Bachrach, Laura Hill, Kellenn Kay, Pamela Holcomb, and Elisa Koff, "The Demography of Out-of-Wedlock Childbearing," in U.S. Department of Health and Human Services, National Center for Health Statistics, "Report to Congress on Out-of-Wedlock Childbearing," DHHS Pub. no. (PHS) 95-1257, (Washington, D.C.: U.S. Government Printing Office, 1995): 105.
12. *Kids Count Data Book: State Profiles of Child Well-Being*, (Baltimore, MD: The Annie E. Casey Foundation, 1995): 125.
13. Kristin A. Moore, Angela Romano, and Cheryl Oakes, *Facts at a Glance*, Washington, D.C.: Child Trends, October 1996.
14. U.S. Bureau of the Census, *Statistical Abstracts of the United States, 1997*, U.S. Government Printing Office, Washington, D.C., 1997.
15. John P. Robinson, "Caring For Kids," *American Demographics*, July, 1989, p. 52.
16. Peter L. Benson, *The Troubled Journey: A Portrait of 6th-12th Grade Youth*. Minneapolis, MN: Search Institute, 1993, p. 84.

17. *The Role of Fathers in America: Attitudes and Behavior*, Gallup national random sample survey conducted for the National Center for Fathering, Shawnee Mission, Kansas, April 1992.
18. Frank F. Furstenberg, Jr., and Christine Winquist Nord, "Parenting Apart: Patterns of Child Rearing After Marital Disruption," *Journal of Marriage and the Family*, (November 1985): 896.
19. Frank Furstenberg and Andrew Cherlin, *Divided Families: What Happens to Children When Parents Part* (Cambridge, MA: Harvard University Press, 1991).
20. Robert Lerman and Theodora Ooms, *Young Unwed Fathers: Changing Roles and Emerging Policies* (Philadelphia, PA: Temple, 1993): 45.
21. Ibid.
22. Frank F. Furstenberg and K. M. Harris, "When and why fathers matter: Impacts of father involvement on children of adolescent mothers." In Robert I. Lerman & Theodora J. Ooms (Eds.), *Young Unwed Fathers.* Philadelphia, PA: Temple University Press, 1993, pp. 117-138.
23. Moore, Kristin A., "Non-marital Childbearing in the United States." In: U.S. Department of Health and Human Services, "Report to Congress on Out-of-Wedlock Childbearing," DHHS Pub. no. (PHS) 95-1257, (Washington, D.C.: U.S. Government Printing Office, 1995): vii.
24. Linda S. Stephens, "Will Johnny See Daddy This Week?" *Journal of Family Issues* 17 (1996): 466-494.
25. National Commission on Children, "Just the Facts: A Summary of Recent Information on America's Children and Their Families," (Washington, D.C.: U.S. Government Printing Office, 1993).
26. Debra Dawson, "Family Structure and Children's Well-Being: Data from the 1988 National Health Survey," *Journal of Marriage and Family* 53 (1991); U.S. Department of Health and Human Services, National Center for Health Statistics, "Survey of Child Health," (Washington, D.C.: U.S. Government Printing Office, 1993).
27. U.S. Department of Health and Human Services, National Center for Health Statistics, "National Health Interview Survey," (Hyattsville, MD: U.S. Government Printing Office, 1988).
28. Irwin Garfinkel and Sara McLanahan, *Single Mothers and Their Children* (Washington, D.C.: Urban Institute Press, 1986); Susan Newcomer and J. Richard Udry, "Parental Marital Status Effects on Adolescent Sexual Behavior," *Journal of Marriage and the Family* (May 1987): 235-240.
29. U.S. Department of Health and Human Services, National Center for Health Statistics, "Survey on Child Health," (Washington, D.C.: U.S. Government Printing Office, 1993).
30. Nicholas Davidson, "Life Without Father," *Policy Review* (1990).
31. Dewey Cornell, et al., "Characteristics of Adolescents Charged with Homicide," *Behavioral Sciences and the Law* 5 (1987): 11-23.

32. M. Eileen Matlock, et al., "Family Correlates of Social Skills Deficits in Incarcerated and Nonincarcerated Adolescents, *Adolescence* 29 (1994): 119-130.
33. Patricia L. McCall and Kenneth C. Land, "Trends in White Male Adolescent Young-Adults and Elderly Suicide: Are There Common Underlying Structural Factors?" *Social Science Research* 23 (1994): 57-81; U.S. Department of Health and Human Services, National Center for Health Statistics, "Survey on Child Health," (Washington, D.C.: U.S. Government Printing Office, 1993).
34. Catherine M. Malkin and Michael E. Lamb, "Child Maltreatment: A Test of Sociobiological Theory," *Journal of Comparative Family Studies* 25 (1994): 121-130.
35. Urie Bronfenbrenner, "What do Families do?" *Family Affairs* (Winter/ Spring 1991): 1-6.
36. Ways and Means Committee, U.S. House of Representatives, *1996 Green Book*. Washington, D.C., 1996, p. 580.
37. Ways and Means Committee, U.S. House of Representatives, *1996 Green Book*. Washington, D.C., 1996, p. 578.
38. See, for example, Kristen A. Moore, Donna Ruane Morrison, Martha Zaslow and Dana A. Glei, *Ebbing and Flowing, Learning and Growing: Family Economic Resources and Children's Development*. Paper presented at the Workshop on Welfare and child Development sponsored by the Board of children and Families of the national Institute of child Health and Development's Family and child Well-Being Network.
39. Thomas M. Guterbock, Ten Chang, Robert E. Emery, and Brian J. Meekins, *Evaluation of The Virginia Fatherhood Media Campaign*, Charlottesville, VA: Center for Survey Research, November 1997.
40. John Gottman, "The Dissolution of the American Family." In: William J. O'Neill, Jr., (ed., *Family: The first Imperative*. Cleveland, OH: The William J. and Dorothy K. O'Neill Foundation, 1995, p. 103.
41. For a further discussion of this idea see: Wade F. Horn and Andrew Bush, *Fathers, Marriage and Welfare Reform*. Indianapolis, IN: The Hudson Institute, 1997.
42. Angela D. Greene and Kristin A. Moore, "Nonresident Father Involvement and Child Outcomes Among Young Children in Families on Welfare," paper presented at the Conference on Father Involvement, October 10-11, 1996, National Institutes of Health, Bethesda, Maryland.

Chapter 6

ꟷ

Myths and Obstacles that Keep Men from Their Families

Armin Brott*

I do a lot of writing about fatherhood—a topic I probably wouldn't have considered if I hadn't become a parent myself. In fact, it's fair to say that my kids are responsible for giving me a new career. Let me take a minute to explain what I mean.

In 1989, when my then wife was pregnant with my oldest child, I made the decision that I was going to cut my work schedule back to part-time and spend the rest or my day taking care of my child. Until then everything in my business career had been going along just fine: I was making a lot of money, I was indispensable to my employer, and I had a pretty good life. But the moment I decided to be less-than-completely traditional, things changed. I told my employer, "I have a modem, a fax, e-mail, and I can be at the office in half an hour if you really need

---

*Armin Brott is a journalist and writer who has written a great deal about father's issues. He has published two books: *The New Father* and *Throwaway Dads: The Myths and Obstacles that Keep Men from Being the Fathers They Want to Be.*

me." But none of that did any good. They were rigid and inflexible. Getting called "Mr. Mom" and having people make fun of me and treat me with suspicion, as though I wasn't serious about my career anymore, were humiliating and infuriating. It gave me a clear, yet sad and disturbing, insight into the true nature of the business world.

I decided, after a while of doing the part-time thing and accepting the humiliation, that I could do better elsewhere, and I began to write about some of the issues I'd dealt with. I wrote about men taking paternity leave, and about the really miserable portrayal of fathers in children's books. And through some incredible statistical miracle, I got the children's book article published in "Newsweek," which, if you're trying to launch a writing career—which I hadn't intended to do—is probably the best place in the world to start. The article attracted a huge amount of attention and I began hearing from people—mostly fathers—all over the country that it really had touched a nerve with them.

I spend a lot of time after that thinking and talking with other men about how the ways our society treats fathers influences the type of relationships fathers have with their children. And over the next several years I identified a number of significant obstacles that men, women, the media, the medical community, and society in general place in the way of fathers who truly want to be involved with their children. Basically, what I'm saying is that while the public and policy makers insist that fathers are abandoning their families, the truth is that men are being driven away. Fatherlessness, then, is far more involuntary than voluntary.

I should mention here that what I've just said, and what I'm going to be talking about here, is a very condensed version of a book that will be out in early 1999 called "Throwaway Dads: The Myths and Obstacles that Keep Men from Being the Fathers They Want to Be." It's basically about how men and women and society essentially conspire to keep men away from their children.

Let's start with money. One of the first obstacles to involved fatherhood is our insane insistence on judging men by what's in their pants. No, not the front. The back: their wallets. Dozens of studies over the course of dozens of years consistently show that women (and men) believe that a guy who is not a good provider is not a good man or a good father. In fact, men and women—in roughly equal numbers—rate a man's ability to provide for his family as one of the top identifiers of being a good father. Fathers' emotional, psychological, and even social contributions to their children—which are far more significant than money could ever be—are largely ignored.

Just to give you a few examples: Kids who grow up with active, involved fathers (and even with those fathers who are at least in the home) do better in school. They tend to be less involved with drugs, less involved with promiscuous sex, have higher self-esteem, and are more empathetic. But instead of focusing on the positive impact fathers have on their children and instead of figuring out how we can encourage fathers to be more involved with their children, we spend all our time talking about collecting money from deadbeat dads or having fathers repay AFDC money that's gone out to welfare women.

In one of his many books, Dr. Warren Farrell points out that women, after becoming mothers, have three options: They can work part-time, they can work full-time, or they can work something in between. Men also have three options: They can go to work, they can go to work, or they can go to work. Now that may be a bit of an exaggeration—exceptions happen, as my situation illustrates—but there is something to what Farrell says. Men's options are greatly curtailed. Wade Horn, who's here today, put it another way: "Emphasizing fatherhood in largely economic terms has helped contribute to its demise. If we want fathers to be more than just money machines, we need a culture that supports their work as teachers, coaches, nurturers, disciplinarians, and moral instructors." Those two sentences should really be on a monument somewhere.

Another barrier to involved fatherhood is in the way the media portrays fathers. On television, we see Homer Simpson and Al Bundy. There's also Bill Cosby and Tim Allen, who, on the surface, seem like involved fathers. But if you look closely, you'll see that they're total buffoons. Their kids are constantly outwitting them and rarely turn to them for serious advice, their wives don't respect them. These images are nearly universal in sitcoms, dramas, and movies. There are a few exceptions, but the general theme is that dad is just another one of the kids, an emasculated authority figure no one really needs to have around. In short, he's superfluous.

Television and print ads amplify this message even more. Products are kid tested and mother approved. Mom will get the stains out with "A-L-L" and Doctor Mom will cure your coughs. The basic message of all this is that dads don't really care. They are not there to answer your questions. They can't solve your problems. Mom is the "true" parent.

We are raising a bunch of little boys who are growing up believing fatherhood is not anything to which he should particularly aspire (who in their right mind would want to be the butt of constant jokes?). And we're raising a bunch of girls who are getting the message from very early on that a man is not necessarily anything you need to have around the house, since you can do it all by yourself.

Other media messages are far more sinister. Just think for a second about John Walsh, of the spokespeople for television's America's Most Wanted. He is constantly talking about the 50,000 kids who are "maimed, raped, and murdered each year in this country." As a parent I can only imagine the agony Walsh and others like him endured when their children were kidnapped and murdered, the simple fact is that Walsh is wildly exaggerating the problem. There aren't anywhere near 50,000 children maimed, raped, and murdered each year. There are about 300. And of the million or so children Walsh and other advocates claim disappear or are abducted each year, well over 90 percent of them were taken by a disgruntled divorced parent or ran away.

The problem is that the media loves a good story and big numbers—even if they're false—sell newspapers and increase viewership. And to help them rivet our attention even more, they've given all these supposed murderers and kidnappers an identity: a man, usually with a mustache, sometimes lurking in the bushes outside a park, but always a man.

These images and misinformation can take a heavy toll. A few years ago I had an experience which I wrote about for an article in the "New York Times." I was in the park with my daughter, who's this gorgeous little angelic thing with blonde hair, and I was pushing her on the swing. A few feet away there was a little girl teetering at the top of a slide and I could see that she was just about to fall backwards down the stairs. It wasn't a particularly heroic gesture, but I reached over and grabbed her out of the air and sat her down. Her mother came over, snatched the kid up, and I heard her asking the girl as she walked away, "Did he hurt you?" It certainly took the wind out of my sails. I wasn't expecting money or a reward, but maybe a "thank you," or a smile, or a nod of appreciation. I've talked to a lot of fathers who have had similar experiences and there's no question that being treated with suspicion for no other reason than being a man, makes them think twice before taking their children to a public park. They don't want to endure the looks, the whispers, and even the 9-1-1 reporting them to the police. As a result, their relationships with their kids suffer.

As I mentioned earlier, some of the most significant obstacles faced by men are erected by the business community. Men are making major strides in changing their careers by taking positions that involve less travel and perhaps passing over promotions. But in a fairly recent study the directors and CEOs of 1,500 major corporations were asked how much time would be reasonable for a man to take off for paternity leave. Over forty percent said none. This goes a long way in explaining why it is that only about three percent of eligible men take advantage of family leave when they have the chance. They don't take it even when it's paid. Yes, a lot of men don't take family leave because it isn't paid and because, if they have to do without one spouse's income, it's better to do without the wife's, who probably makes less anyway. But the biggest reason men don't take family leave is that they're afraid of committing career suicide.

And then there's what goes on in the medical community. In hospitals, starting with the OB/GYN visits, men are not made to feel particularly welcome. They are not encouraged to ask questions. They are treated as spectators and when their babies are born, they are not encouraged to go to the pediatrician's office. It's so hard to get a pediatrician appointment after five o'clock, which is when a lot of men realistically need to be able to take their kids to the doctor. There's no reason why a kid can't go after five o'clock. A recent study in England found a dramatic increase in the number of fathers who brought their children to pediatricians' offices when those offices offered extended hours.

Taken together, all these obstacles form what I like to call "the Other Glass Ceiling." It's a barrier that's similar in a way to the one that keeps women from advancing in the workplace. But while we've come a long way toward dismantling women's glass ceiling, men's is still very much intact. Interestingly, though, both of these two transparent barriers are inextricably related and exist for nearly the same reason: power. Men are reluctant to give up their dominance in the workplace, while women are just as reluctant to give up their dominance at home. But until we start recognizing that fathers have a unique and vital role in their children's lives and until we, as a society, start encouraging—and allowing—men to be more involved with their children, women won't ever be free to take on more responsible positions outside the home. The day that fatherhood becomes as synonymous with love and nurturing as motherhood is we'll know we've made some real progress.

Part II

Women in Business

In Section Two, four very successful women entrepreneurs relate their experience of breaking into the formerly male-dominated business world, and discuss the sometimes rocky paths that took them to where they are now. First, Louise Woerner, a 20-year veteran in the health care field with undergraduate and graduate degrees in business, recalls overcoming the initial hurdle of her gender and offers specific strategies to woman-owned businesses on how to be successful in the 21st Century. Next, Judi Schindler, a small business owner and an active member of the National Association of Women Business Owners, observes the decades-long progress women have made in business from her own unique vantage point as a successful entrepreneur. Third, Deborah Mancini, who began her company with only a small amount of cash and a business plan scribbled on a restaurant placemat, discusses the importance of building solid business relationships and utilizing mentors in order to succeed in a competitive business world. Finally, Frances Smith, who runs a large non-profit consumer group, offers an interesting glimpse into the unique challenges for women in non-profit organizations to raise funds, exert influence in public policy matters, and increase the visibility of the organization. While the experiences of all four women vary, their stories share a common theme of determination and success, which serves as an inspiration to all those for whom they have blazed a trail.

Chapter 7

ꙮ

Women Entrepreneurs

Louise Woerner*

Entrepreneurial activity is the underpinning of a great American economy. Today, we are thinking about enterprise as part of two global phenomena that are converging: the marketization of the world that we have seen over the last 10 years, with the reform in the former Soviet nations to more market-based economies, and the global empowerment of women.

As a 20-year veteran who started in the health care field, I have a unique perspective. Our company, Health Care Resources (HCR), is in three lines of business. We were the first home health care organization certified by the State of New York, and we continue to deliver home health services. Those services now include complimentary alternative services in addition to nursing and the five types of therapy with which

---

*Louise Woerner is the owner of Health Care Resources (HCR). Ms. Woerner has consulted internationally in health care and is founder of the Friends of the National Institute of Nursing Research, a Director of the National Women's Hall of Fame, and active in women's organizations.

you would be most familiar. We also have a health information product line; in the industry, we call them demand-based systems but they are really telephone support systems to call people that have the 20 ambulatory care sensitive diseases. For example, if you have an arthritis condition and you have to manage your health care, we can call you or you can call us so that you can avoid a hospital stay or an emergency room trip.

Through our Washington, D.C. branch, we conduct public policy work. We have contracts with organizations such as the Centers for Disease Control, the National Institutes of Health, the Agency for Health Care Policy Research, and the U.S. Public Health Association. We support the Surgeon General on breast cancer and cervical cancer tracking. We review laws to report to the Congress on issues related to smoking and health around the United States.

How did we get there? It has been a track very similar for other women. As someone who earned her undergraduate and graduate degrees in business, I expected to know quite a lot about what it took to be in business. My first experiences told me that maybe there was more to learn than I had thought. I had prepared a more detailed business plan. I had monthly projections for the first year; I had quarterly projections for the next 3 years; and I had annual projections for the rest of the 5 years. I was ready to talk to bankers. I was trying to borrow $10,000. Today, you can borrow that on your credit cards; then, it was quite a challenge because I did not have a father or a husband who could co-sign my note. I was turned down by several banks. It was quite difficult. I had my business plan and I was confident I was going to be approved. Finally, after being turned down at four or five places, I went to a bank that was suggested to me—Chase Bankers, which was moving to upstate New York. I met with George Burton, who said: "I can't lend you less than $40,000 because it costs too much to do the paperwork, and I don't have time to hear your business plan." It was a big step for me, but I decided I had better take the bird in the hand.

To be successful in the 21st Century, four strengths are needed. People who are successful in business must be able to assimilate a tremendous amount of information available today. You will have a very difficult time if you cannot sort and assimilate the important facts. The possession of a vast amount of energy, both physical and intellectual, also will be required. You also must have a high tolerance for risk and failure. Finally, you need to have a strong desire to do something of value, as well as to be successful.

First, running a business requires a tremendous amount of information assimilation. The CEO and owner is the visionary of an organization. You need to update your vision as you go or to check your vision against the context of the environment—what changes are happening and what new information is developing that may cause you to fine tune your thinking. Most entrepreneurs are voracious readers. Most use the Internet but most also read a lot, and not only about business. *Fortune* magazine is read by many entrepreneurs. There are stories not only of businesses but of people. I never took an Evelyn Woods course but I probably should have. Scanning information for issues of interest is very important, just as is being in contact with people in the know and with others who can inform your thinking.

It is very important to make the effort to be out and about. It is very easy, particularly when starting a business, to sit at your desk. Today, when you can use technology to such a degree, it may be not as important, but being out, getting information, talking to people who are knowledgeable is still very valuable.

Assimilating information has led to my vision for the future of our company, and it is a different vision from what other people have seen. We have added complimentary alternative treatments to our practice. In 1993, for the first time, more complimentary alternative treatments were done than traditional western treatments. This data, along with the changing numbers of complimentary practitioners, the science behind complimentary practitioners, and the addition by the National Institutes of Health of an office in complimentary alternative medicine, caused me to think about one of the divisions of our company and to embark on a new direction. It is not the direction that everyone sees in home care but it is one that we are finding very useful. There are great amounts of information to think about to fine-tune your own vision.

Next, running a business requires physical stamina as well as mental stamina in life-long learning. It requires creativity because the environment is constantly changing; that part is fun. The physical stamina required to do all the things in business also is very important. For example, the president of my company is Barbara Robinson. We have worked together for almost the entire time I have been in business. I was able to attract her after two or three years of being in business. We were putting together business proposals and it was very hard early on in the business. I had dropped her off after 3:00 a.m., after working late on getting a proposal together for a client. As I dropped her off, I asked her, without realizing how it might sound, if she could come in a little earlier in the morning. She looked at me and said, _Would you mind if I took time to change my clothes?_ Maybe it was adrenaline, but it had not occurred to me that a little sleep was needed because I was running on such an energy high. It has been the secret of my success to have a tremendous amount of physical stamina. Physical stamina and intellectual energy are very important.

Successful business persons must also have a high tolerance for risk and failure. Failure feels terrible when it happens. People talk about normal business cycles, bad years as well as good years. However, it does not feel very normal as a business cycle when you are in the middle of it. Among business people, though, failure is a badge of honor if you do not get taken out altogether. In the Rochester community, one of the great successes is Max Farish. He is a multi- multi-millionaire who received, a few years before I did, an award. When I received the award, he was there to celebrate with me. He wanted to know if I had the same stature as he to receive the award. He said, "What's the most money that you've ever lost?" I answered, "Well, one year, I lost $4 million." He said, "You've been tested." It was very interesting to me. I had not really thought about business cycles. Max Farish assumed that I had some degree of success, but he wondered at what price it had been earned, and how hard it had been for me to achieve that success. It was interesting to me that he saw that as the real sign of success. He has been very supportive of me since, and I think I was an appropriate colleague for that award.

Values are also very much a part of success in business. There has been an unfortunate concern about how people make money, the price they extract, and whether it is good for society. When you are doing something to make money and to make a difference, it should have value. When you create value and deliver a needed product, you focus on that first and the money will follow. Some people use the excuse that it is just a business decision to do things that might be considered unacceptable behavior. Those are really not good business decisions, particularly not in the long-term. Some people are willing to make a difference. I just returned from working on NATO expansion issues with the United States Government and the Atlantic Treaty Association. We were working in Bulgaria and had the opportunity to hear from Lech Wolenska and Shimon Peres about their struggles. When you hear what people at that level are willing to do, it certainly makes me feel that business is the easy track.

Today, most entrepreneurs and business people have a strong sense of values. There are many hidden heroes in our country who have built this country and made it great. Henry Ford said that a business that makes nothing but money is a poor kind of business.

Today, women business owners are a huge part of the economy. Over the last ten years, you have seen women experience high growth rates in the non-traditional sectors. In most business discussions with women entrepreneurs, there are women manufacturers, women in construction, women in transportation, and women in wholesale trade in global industries.

If entrepreneurship is not fun, you should not do it. My business has many challenges, joys, and failures. I have grown differently from anything I could have foreseen when I started out 20 years ago. I would do it all again and I would encourage you all to do it too. Women entrepreneurs have made tremendous strides over the last two decades and we look forward to the next two decades. There are outstanding opportunities that we hope we have been part of helping to create. As Mark Twain said, "Twenty years from now, you'll be more disappointed by the things you didn't do than by the things that you did." I encourage you to sail forward into the 21st century. We'll look for you there.

Chapter 8

ᴥ

Women's Enterprise: The Coming of Age

Judi Schindler*

As a business owner for almost two decades and an active member of the National Association of Women Business Owners (NAWBO) for the same time period, I have had a chance to observe the progress women have made at close range. And I would like to share some of those observations.

Let's start by looking at the numbers. In 1972, the portion of firms owned by women was less than five percent. Ten years later, it was 15 to 20 percent. By 1996, according to the National Foundation for Women Business Owners, there were nearly 8 million women-owned firms, representing 36 percent of all businesses in the country and providing employment for 18.5 million people—one out of every four U.S. company workers. And if that is not impressive enough, one more number is: in 1996, women-owned businesses generated close to $2.3 trillion in sales.

---

*Judi Schindler is founder of Schindler Communications, Inc. She is active in the National Association of Women Business Owners. She is a frequent speaker, both locally and nationally, on marketing and women's enterprise.

To understand these statistics, I would like to take a step back—to set the stage—to tell you how it was so you can appreciate how it is. I particularly want to do this for younger women readers who are probably not aware what it was like when women my age were starting out—back in the dark ages—the 60's.

My college major was journalism, which made me something of an oddity in those days. Back then most women majored in elementary education. And the vast majority dropped out before graduation—many to marry, which was the *real* goal after all. But I chose journalism. I wanted a career. Specifically I wanted to be a police reporter like my two role models—the only women I knew who were not teachers or nurses. I am speaking, of course, of Brenda Star and Lois Lane.

When I was a senior in college, I participated in a formal round table discussion with other women—all journalism majors—all preparing for careers. The main focus of our discussion was: "what would you do if the man you married did not want you to work?" This was a serious conversation—the subject of heated debate.

After graduation, I began looking for a job in the help wanted ads. In those days, there were two separate listings—one for men and one for women. This sounds shocking today, but the *Chicago Tribune* classified ads did not go gender neutral until the early 70s.

As for women business owners, a good percentage were widows who wound up taking over the family business out of necessity. My mother was one. She took over the family shoe store. Katherine Graham of the Washington Post was another. I recently read her biography, "A Personal History," in which she is quite frank about how unprepared she was (in the early 60s) to take over the Post Company and how insecure and intimidated she felt around the executives who reported to her. She even admits to crying when a subordinate criticized her managerial skills. It was unthinkable then for a woman to own anything larger than a book store or candy shop or other marginally profitable businesses.

Part of the problem was with us. We did not grow up with the idea of owning a business. We did not receive the proper education for it. We did not position ourselves properly in our careers. We did not want to do anything that was unladylike or might offend people. Most of all, we did not want to take risks.

And part of the problem was with men. They wanted us at home taking care of their needs. A working wife was embarrassing. It meant the husband was not a good provider. And, frankly, they did not take us very seriously on business issues. *"Now, don't you bother your pretty little head."*

Then came the 70's—EEOC, the National Organization of Women, *MS.* Magazine, rap sessions, consciousness raising, bell bottoms and unisex dressing and, of course, unisex classified ads. As if all this wasn't enough to push women out of the home and into the job market, economic forces were also at play—an accelerating divorce rate, inflation and a recession.

So women came pouring back into the business world, both as employees and entrepreneurs. A new era of women business owners was born—women who started businesses on purpose rather than through an accident of fate.

For the next 10 years, essentially two types of women started businesses. Those who were over qualified for the job market and those who were under qualified. The over qualified, like myself, were the ones who had been working all along and had managed to rise above the administrative ranks—primarily in areas such as marketing, communications, human resources, and the health care industry.

Through diligence, perseverance and talent we had reached the exalted heights of middle management or its equivalent. One day we looked around and realized we had gone as far as we were going to go. The phrase "glass ceiling" was coined. And we were smack dab against it. So we started a business. Usually as a consultant in a field that was related to our experience.

One woman I knew in those days, Karen Gibson, started out as a hospital nurse. For years she was frustrated with hospital bureaucracy, egomaniac physicians and a health care system that often impeded good patient care. Having topped out as a nurse, she began looking for another way she could utilize her nursing skills and credentials. As a result, she and a partner opened a nurse-practitioner office and began seeing patients on their own—to administer injections, change surgical dressings and provide other nursing services outside a hospital or doctor's office. That initial practice grew to 500 employees and three profit centers: a relief staffing service, a nurse registry as well as the nursing practice.

Karen's story is fairly typical. In the 70s, human resource managers became head hunters or started a temporary employment service. Association executives became meeting planners. Executive secretaries started secretarial services. Public relations people started public relations firms.

On the flip side, there was that other group of women who started businesses because they were under qualified for the job market. These were ex-teachers, social workers and home makers. Many were divorced. They were the "re-entry housewives," and they wanted careers either as a way of finding fulfillment, a necessary paycheck, or both.

Few doors opened for them. They may have had brains, education and organizational skills, but on paper they still did not have the credentials for a managerial position. So one day they got a great idea for a business. The following are a few examples of women who fall into this category.

Judy Aronson, a high school friend of mine, was an assistant buyer in a department store and a substitute school teacher before she retired to have children. Later, she was on vacation in Florida when she got the idea to distribute sea shells—a business at which she enjoyed a modest income.Then one day she saw a simple belt that combined leather thongs and a large scallop shaped shell. So she drilled a few holes in one of her own shells, ran some cord threw it and went into the belt business—which was later expanded to belts and accessories. Today, she has a national network of distributors and her product line is sold all over the country under the label "Shell Game." She tells me she was in Rome once, and saw a woman wearing one of her belts.

Another woman I know, Linda Hughes, an ex-social worker, began importing—first a line of giftware she had seen in Japan and later rubber bands from Thailand—thus beginning the first of several businesses she went on to own.

These early entrepreneurs, regardless of whether they were under qualified or over qualified for the job market, had one thing in common. Their businesses were primarily low-risk, easy-entry enterprises. It does not take a major capital investment to be a consultant. Essentially, you need letterhead, a desk, phone and enough savings to cover your personal expenses for a few months. Judy and Linda's businesses were equally low risk. They both started in their homes with a couple thousand dollars worth of inventory.

In the 80s, the phenomenon of the re-entry housewife was over. And the glass ceiling had suffered some major cracks. Women were becoming executive vice presidents, division heads, even CEOs. At the same time, a new breed of women were becoming entrepreneurs. Some were younger women who had grown up with fewer self-imposed limitations and less restrictive conceptions about their role in life. Others were older, but had been emboldened by the success of their predecessors.

Regardless of age, what distinguishes the new breed is they are *risk takers*.

Leslie Hindman launched Leslie Hindman Auctioneers in 1982 after raising $250,000 from eight outside investors. In short order, she built her company to the largest art and antique auction house in Chicago. She recently sold the venture to Sotheby's for a very substantial profit to the delight of her investors as well as herself.

Susan Mravka was Vice President of Marketing for a large company that provided third-party technical service for computer components. One day her boss told her they were re-structuring and she was going to have to move to San Antonio. She opted not to move and instead, she came back to Chicago and invested her savings in creating a similar company of her own. Without a single customer, she signed a lease for an 8,000-square-foot facility. In 1996 Susan had 100 employees and revenue of $6.25 million from three businesses—component repair, temporary staffing of computer technicians and a software development business. This year, she sold two of those companies for a combination of stock and cash.

Rachel Hubka also went at risk. Rachel was a divorcee with small children when she went to work for a school bus company as the office manager. Ten years later she had risen through the ranks to become general manager. It was then that the owners told her they were closing the company. If she wanted to start a similar business on her own, they would lease her the buses. Rachel took the risk and created not only a profitable business but one that has been cited nationally as a leader in the welfare-to-work movement. Hillary Clinton paid homage to Rachel and Rachel's Bus Company in her book "It Takes a Village."

In 1988, Shirley Gross-Moore, an African American, was offered the opportunity to buy a failing, badly managed Dodge dealership in, of all places, the lily-white suburb of Barrington, Ill. Shirley not only accepted the challenge and turned the dealership around, she paid off her loans to Chrysler ahead of schedule.

In my opinion, the risk takers have taken women's enterprise to a higher level. They have a different mind set. They are not just employing themselves. They are building enterprises that stand on their own. They are making an investment that ultimately will pay a handsome return. They are creating wealth.

This brings us to the 90s—the newest phase in women's enterprise—*reaping the rewards*. I belong to a sub group within NAWBO—an exchange group—some 17 women who meet every five or six weeks to talk about their businesses, to share new ideas or information and to profit from each other's experiences. Since the group got started some 12 or 13 years ago, we have had four members who cashed out—sold their businesses for sums large enough that they now play golf or sit on the beach all day.

One sold to her daughter in a long-planned leveraged buyout. One sold to an employee. And the others sold to large companies from their own industries. While, personally, I am not interested in retiring, the ability to cash out is the final proof that you have built an entity that stands on its own. It is proof that the investment you have made (both in money and in sweat) has paid off.

There is another 90's phenomenon that I would like to mention: mother-daughter businesses. I know of dozens. Some are businesses that were started by the mother and daughter as partners. For example, Exchange Business Service, which manages associations and provides other business supports, was started by Sandra Gidley and her daughter Debbie in 1992. As the business has grown, two other daughters, Sheila and Susan, joined the company.

In other cases, the mother started the business, and the daughter joined much later.

Gail Izenstark started her company Direct Mail Source, in 1980. The company provides a full scope of mailing services and data base management. Her daughter Debbie joined the business some five years ago. She has helped expand the business and given Gail the opportunity to take a little time off.

Marie Gebbie, who founded and built Action Bag Company, has since retired and left her company to be managed by two daughters—one as president, the other as marketing director.

The interesting thing about mother-daughter businesses is that the partners seem to get along better than fathers and sons. I once asked a psychologist why this was so. He explained that fathers and sons compete with each other, while mothers and daughter support each other. When a daughter succeeds, the mother takes vicarious pleasure in her success. When a son succeeds, the father just feels old. Thus we have yet another kind of reward we are seeing in the 90s—the psychological reward of being able to pass the torch to your daughter and to see her and the business both flourish.

Let's review how far women have come as business owners. From the accidental entrepreneur (the widow), to the pioneers who were seeking alternative employment, to the risk takers, and finally to those who are reaping the rewards either by selling their businesses or by handing them down to their daughters. What does the future hold? Are there any new mountains to climb? We have proven we can start a business, grow a business and cash out. We are in traditional businesses and non- traditional businesses. What else is there?

Few of us have yet crossed the line from small business to big business. While there have been women who have started or grown mega businesses such as Kathryn Graham, Liz Claiborne, Mary Kay, Donna Karan, none of their companies are currently listed on the Fortune 500. The only two companies started by women on this year's list are Mattel and Estee Lauder. With all the women business owners I know, I frankly can not think of a single one who has taken her business public. Only one I know is franchising her business across the country. And I certainly have not heard of any women out there leading hostile takeovers.

But the story of women's enterprise is not fully written. We are really just beginning. It has taken us 20 years to get on an equal footing with male enterprises of our size. But I do not believe it will take that long for us to break through to big business and the Fortune 500.

In "Megatrends for Women," the authors John Naisbitt and Patricia Aburdene quote Edward Moldt of the Wharton School who says, "Women's attitudes about team building and consensus are much more geared to leading through growth stages of business than men." He says it's a stair-step kind of process. "You get comfortable with running a business at a certain level and say, 'Gee, I can do more than that.' Then you step up to another size."

Professor Moldt adds his view that women will soon develop businesses in the $50 million to $100 million-a-year category and there will be billion-dollar women-owned businesses as well.

Naisbitt and Aberdeen point the way for this business development by indicating likely high-growth areas—areas where women have already made strides. Among the industries they cite are health care, child care and elder care, technology and the sciences, finance, food, fashion and the arts.

Undoubtedly there will be other avenues the authors could not possibly predict in 1992 when they wrote their book. Certainly, the Internet offers new opportunities for starting mega businesses because it reduces the cost of marketing and distribution while increasing its customer base exponentially every day. Technology is opening all kinds of new doors, and women will be there to take advantage of each new opportunity.

The future is very exciting. It holds endless possibilities—particularly for those of you who are just getting started today. I wish all of you well. I am confident you will succeed because millions of women have forged the way on your behalf. We will be watching you. We will be cheering you on. And like mothers observing daughters, we will share vicariously in your success.

Chapter 9

ℵ

Life of a Start Up

DEBORAH MANCINI*

I remember the day I first began to think about starting my own firm. It was September 29, 1996. I had called a friend of mine, Irene Palmer, to let her know that I wasn't that happy at my present company. She asked me why I wasn't going to open my own firm. I immediately thought, I can't do that, but the more I thought about it, the more I realized I could do it. That night I went out to dinner with my husband and discussed it with him. During dinner, we began to write down all the things I needed to do and all the people I could draw on to help me on the back of a placemat from the restaurant. That was my first business plan.

Once I made up my mind to pursue the dream of owning my own business, nothing could stop me. I conducted most of my research on the Internet and read every book I could get my hands on at the public library. I also took classes at the Women's Business Center in Washington

---

*Deborah Mancini is founder of Mancini Technical Recruiting (MTR). A key element of MTR's operating culture is community investment.

and I met with representatives through the Small Business Administration (SBA), and the Small Business District of Columbia, SBDC, in the DC area. My goal was to get as much advice as possible so that I would make fewer mistakes. I had been in the same industry since 1988, so I knew the industry but what I needed to learn was all the other ingredients that make a business run smoothly.

The big day came. I gave notice to my employer. I had assumed that they would ask me to leave since I would be competing against them, but instead they asked for a month notice and had me transition my accounts during that time. They also allowed me extra time off to set up my office and get things in place.

I started Mancini Technical Recruiting on February 3, 1997. My firm is a permanent placement company specializing in the technical industry. The first three to four months were grueling. It was so hard to stay positive when nothing seemed to be "jelling". I either had a candidate who absolutely loved the company, but the company didn't want to hire them, or a company loved the candidate, but the candidate didn't want the company. In my industry, you can have a lot of openings with employers, but unless you fill them successfully, you won't make money. This was definitely the hardest time. My husband was wonderful and so supportive. He reminded me why I had wanted to do this and always helped me to focus on what needed to be done.

I think the advice I would give someone who is starting his or her own business is to do your homework. Even though I spent endless hours researching, talking to other business owners in my field, and taking classes, there were still some things I wasn't prepared for. Also, I think you need a sense of humor and a good support network to really be successful at this. My husband was wonderful every step of the way and even to this day, after he gets home from a long day at work, he helps me with the clerical work.

I am not sure I am the best one to give advice to someone in business but if asked, I would say to remember to treat everyone like your best client. Whether it is a salesperson trying to sell you something, your vendor, or any one else with whom you come in contact. I have done this and everything has come back to me twofold. An applicant offered to do my homepage for free because he liked me. Someone else tried to sell me a resume tracking system over the phone. I explained that I was a start up and couldn't possibly spend that kind of money at this time.

He asked me if I would be interested in beta testing the program for them and recommending the changes. So now I have the database for free. There are still a lot of people in the world with a big heart but unless you treat people with kindness, you may never know who they are.

As I mentioned, I have been in the same industry for about 10 years but I come from a family of entrepreneurs so I think this might have always been in my "blood".

I think that corporate America has forgotten to hire people who will take on the responsibilities of ownership. In the companies I have worked for there were many people who could get the job done, but yet I seem to accomplish more on my own. It is very hard to teach others a sense of urgency. I like the fact that if I tell my clients it will be done—I know it will be because I am doing it.

I left my permanent corporate job because my company was not flexible. Since then I have seen companies that let mothers work at home, but it seems that working at home means taking a pay cut. I think that women can handle both children and working. I just chose not to put my child in day care. I have someone helping me on a part time basis but I wanted to create a schedule so I could spend lunchtime with my kids. I want to take them on a walk after lunch and put them down for a nap. Then the babysitter can watch them for a few hours.

I also have to say that as a woman, I feel very blessed. Women are very kind to each other and I have two mentors (both women) who are in my industry and who have more experience in their own business than I do. They have held my hand every step of the way and even shared some of their secrets with me. I am not convinced that this would have happened if they were men. But my husband might disagree with me.

As I begin my second year, I look back on my first year in business with pride. I made it. I do realize, though, that many firms fail either during the first year or during the first five years. So I am sure I still have a few obstacles ahead of me. I constantly strive to stay informed and read as much as I can. I have also noticed myself rereading some of the books on starting a business as my focus has changed from starting a business to growing a business. For me, the jump into owning my own business was one of the best things I have ever done.

*****

Mancini Technical Recruiting, a certified Women Owned Enterprise, is an executive search firm specializing in technical placement throughout the United States. Deborah Mancini, the owner, has been in the placement industry since 1988.

Chapter 10

Directing a Non-Profit Organizaton

Frances B. Smith*

I am Executive Director of Consumer Alert, a non-profit consumer group. Consumer Alert is known as a free market consumer group, to differentiate itself. Our mission is to point to the value of a market economy in benefitting consumers through increasing consumer choice and competition, which can lead to lower prices and, in turn, to advances in technology that improve health and safety. This mission puts us on the other side of many issues from the "traditional consumer groups" that push for more government regulation for every perceived consumer problem and consumer issue. We have a philosophical base. Although Consumer Alert is a non-profit organization, I can empathize with many of the issues relating to entrepreneurship and start-up situations.

---

*Frances B. Smith is Executive Director of Consumer Alert, a national consumer group with headquarters in Washington, DC. She is coordinator of the National Consumer Coalition, a group of 25 market-oriented national and state level organizations representing 3.9 million consumers, which focuses on consumer issues in the policy arena.

I joined Consumer Alert three years ago. I would not describe it as a start-up because Consumer Alert was an older organization; it was more of a friendly takeover. The organization was founded in 1977. For most of its history, it was located in a small town in California. It had a very energetic, charismatic, bright founder who throughout her leadership did not pay herself a salary. The organization was perceived as a California organization—a regional organization more than a national consumer organization with individual members in all 50 states.

When I came on board, the organization had moved to a suburb of Washington, D.C. not easily accessible to a subway line. The organization had not had an executive director in over six months. The previous person had worked on Governor Allen's campaign and went with the administration in a fairly high-level appointed position. The policy analyst who was on board bailed out before I joined the organization. I took over the organization with $2,500 in the bank and a lease agreement that extended for another 3-6 months. We had some equipment leases. I had a small payroll to meet, but a payroll nonetheless. I was not only in a friendly takeover but in a turnaround situation. I was philosophically committed to the principles of the organization. In fact, I had thought of starting a consumer group that would be based on these same principles. I had written a proposal and had started shopping the proposal and more and more people said there is an organization very similar to what you would like to start. I got in touch with the people at Consumer Alert and told them my ideas, which were somewhat different from the Board as to where I thought a consumer organization should go. We reached an agreement, they gave me the green light, and I joined the organization.

In the latter part of 1994, we had no money and fairly large commitments that I could not get out of right away. Also, there was some isolation as we were located in a suburb and it was difficult to get to meetings; it would usually take an hour and a half round trip to come to a meeting by car. Our visibility in Washington was very, very low. Besides the low financial visibility, the organization had not increased its political visibility since its founding. Its clout in Washington was cause for concern to some people so I sought emergency funding. I began with a crisis-funding plan and tried to develop a longer-term strategic plan not only for funding but for carrying out the mission of the organization. I had been associated with the public policy world in Washington so I called on allies and people were very helpful. I called the head of a very successful think tank and asked for help. I told him that we did not have any money, and that I needed funds right away to continue operations. I explained the very important purpose of the organization, and our great potential. On his own, he wrote a letter to his 500 largest donors and asked them to consider helping. I naively wrote a letter for him, sent it over for his approval, and he called and said, "Fran, I write my own letters, thank you." His letter was much more forceful than mine. That was the kind of help that was needed.

The membership is several thousand individual members. We did not have the funds to expand the membership through direct mail campaigns so I started searching for ways in my strategic vision of what Consumer Alert could become—for ways to increase our visibility and clout without being heavily dependent on non-existent capital for direct mail. One approach was to look at what groups on the other side of the political spectrum were doing. One model was an umbrella organization of groups known as the Consumer Federation of America. Consumer Federation of America does not have individual members; it has groups such as unions at local and state levels and other like-minded organizations.

This year, I formed the National Consumer Coalition, which is an on-going coalition of market-oriented groups: think tanks, activist groups, grassroots groups, including three seniors groups. We have 25 members right now and represent 3.9 million people because of the large number of seniors in the three groups. That sounds better than Consumer Alert—it is better to represent several thousand people. The National Consumer Coalition focuses on consumer issues in the policy arena and has various issue areas and subgroups. I have only formed two subgroups so far and two more are in formation. We ask the think tanks and others to focus on the consumer implications of some of the policy issues. We also give them a way to represent consumers in testifying and commenting. For example, the Federal Trade Commission held public hearings on privacy issues on the Internet. We had a think tank representative appear on four panels as a consumer representative for the National Consumer Coalition. I recently was asked to meet with Office of Management and Budget personnel on an issue. I went armed with the knowledge that seven or eight members of our National Consumer Coalition also supported Consumer Alert's position.

The strengths of Consumer Alert lie in some of the history. Over the years, Consumer Alert has focused on some critical consumer issues in the public policy process. For example, in the early 1980s, the organization was against the air bag mandate; its position was that consumers should have the choice of whether to buy a car with an airbag. Moreover, not enough research had been done. As you know, the position established many years ago has been vindicated with research. Air bags do pose a risk to certain groups of people: small children (under the age of 12) and small adults. That is an example of an issue where Consumer Alert was way ahead of the curve.

On food safety issues, Consumer Alert had a very strong program. For many years, Consumer Alert had pointed out how food irradiation provides one answer to the question of food safety because it can narrowly irradiate food borne diseases such as E. Coli and salmonella. Food groups on the other side were pushing for more government regulation; many of those groups, particularly a group called Food and Water, would threaten even if a company representative planned to attend a conference on irradiation. This group would send letters threatening boycotts and would have their grassroots people protest outside of the organization. It is only with the outbreak of E. Coli relating to hamburgers—Hudson's Hamburgers and a huge recall—that irradiation has become a focus, and even some of the food industry groups are beginning to explore that as a possibility. At Consumer Alert, we try to argue based on science. We have a very good scientific advisory group which is based on sound science, sound economic principles, and how consumers benefit from many of the processes and technology.

Consumer Alert is now much more financially stable, although not at the stage where it can expand enormously. For the first time ever, there is a 6-month reserve. In many cases, non-profits are advised to have 6-month reserve accounts to even out the flow of donors and membership dues. We have about the same number of members. We can expand further although I am still investigating ways to do that. With the success of the National Consumer Coalition, that may be the way to go as opposed to engaging in heavy direct mail campaigns. In terms of visibility, we have been very pleased. There have been some very talented policy analysts who have helped us enormously, and we may have had our first breakthrough with the networks recently in television appearances and interviews. I see the future of Consumer Alert as one where we are constantly going to have to maintain our credibility. We have received funding from member dues, individual contributions, private foundations—which has been a breakthrough in the last two and a one-half years—and from corporations. To corporations, we send proposals explaining what Consumer Alert does and what its plans are. Do you want to support us? We do absolutely no project work and yet we constantly have to hold things up to a very high standard. Some have said you should not accept corporate funding. However, if there are enlightened corporations that believe a market economy benefits consumers, we should accept the funding.

The major challenges I see are continuing to build visibility, continuing to build the clout that we can exert on public policy issues, and to get into a financial position where needed expansion in some of the issue areas can be accomplished.

Part III

Women in the Military

Women's role in the military is currently a very controversial topic, and the papers included here reflect that controversy. Four women—three career officers in the Army, Navy, and Air Force, and one chaplain in the Army—provide their assessment of women's job performance in the military. Air Force Colonel Lorry Fenner contends that diversity in the military contributes to military effectiveness, is compatible with mission accomplishment, and that the very character of our democracy demands that women be accepted into all branches of the armed services. Similarly, both Army Colonel Barbara Lee and Air Force pilot Linda Heid assert that, contrary to some people's perceptions, women have always been an effective part of our military and that even with their recently added responsibilities, military women want to and can succeed on their own merits and qualifications. In stark contrast to these positive assessments, Reverend Marie de Young, an Army chaplain, posits that many women who have served in the armed forces have gained promotions, assignments, and success through the use of quotas, political leveraging, and media pressure. She chastises the military, the media, and the legal system for exaggerating the physical abilities, accomplishments, and military potential of women beyond their demonstrated records, and she urges women to submit to the same standards of performance as men and to compete based on merit rather than on personal aspirations for glory. While these views are contradictory and certainly controversial, Reverend deYoung offers a unique counterpoint to Officers Fenner, Lee, and Heid, and gives the reader an interesting and unexpected viewpoint to reflect upon.

The ideas expressed in these essays are those of the authors and do not represent an official position of the U.S. military branches in which the authors serve or the offices in which they serve.

Chapter 11

ꕥ

There Then, Where Now? Military Women in the 21st Century

LT. COL. LORRY M. FENNER, USAF*

My mom, in our family, demonstrated a woman could be the head of a household. She was a very strong woman and she was a role model for my sister and me and my younger brothers. She showed us that a woman could take care of everything when the father was off at war or in the hospital for extensive periods of time, both in the United States and Overseas—in the Philippine Islands during the Vietnam War. She grew up in Detroit, had a high school education and did not have a lot of experience with places like the Philippines during a war. My father demonstrated that he thought his daughters could do just about anything. I did not find out until later that he did not think other women could do just about anything, only his daughters. I also realized later

---

*Lorry M. Fenner is a Lieutenant Colonel in the Air force. She has a doctorate in military history from the University of Michigan. She is currently on the faculty of the National War College in the Department of National Securities Strategy.

that my mom, despite role-modeling as a strong woman in the household, was understandably trying to encode standard social behavior—girls did laundry and boys mowed the lawn—in her children. She told us one thing—current gender ideology or mythology—but showed us another—cultural realities.

With this kind of background, both she and I are amazed that I turned out the way I did. It was only later that I realized I did not get to play sports in high school because my school years predated Title IX mandates that girls/women have equal athletic opportunities. Although I would have been qualified to attend the Air Force Academy, women were not allowed to attend then. I could not get a four-year Air Force ROTC scholarship because women could not be pilots and only pilot candidates got four-year scholarships then, even though I had completed ground school as a Civil Air Patrol cadet. It was also unusual then that a woman would be a cadet colonel when I earned that rank (the Spaatz Award in that organization). Nor could I, even though band members were ready to elect me, be a drum major for my high school in 1974. Instead, I would have had to be a "majorette" and we did not have those. I also did not realize then that my possible futures were probably wider than being a nurse—I am more suited to being a doctor or lawyer, a secretary (I refused, to my own detriment, to learn how to type) or a teacher, which I am now. I did not realize then that I should have been more able to aspire to follow through on many possibilities—athletics, the Academy, ROTC, medical school, or law school. These possibilities do not seem so radical now. I did not perceive myself to be radical then, before I came into the military.

Most military women are not radical feminists because we typically do not recruit them, nor do they typically aspire to join the military. So it is not the radical feminists in the military who are beating up the four star admirals and generals. In fact, I do not think most military women are very political at all. I believe this is especially true for enlisted women.

In any case, I became more radical when the military had the wisdom to send me to a civilian graduate school. At first I avoided type-casting. I would not study women's history; I would not study social history; I would not study cultural history; I would study military and political history because that was what I wanted to do—what male officers would do. However, as I studied political and military history, I found more and more women in my historical research and I was as surprised as the next person. My dissertation's title is "Ideology and Amnesia: The Public Debate on Women in the American Military, 1940-1973." It is about the public debate, and not what happened on Capital Hill or in the halls of the Pentagon. It is about what happened among the American citizens and in the public's view—at least of the literate and conscious American public during that time period.

The central questions of the dissertation are about citizenship and civil-military relations. I discuss military culture in the respect that it might be divergent from our civil society and that would be dangerous for our country. If there is any experiment going on here, and here I echo Defense Secretary Cohen's remarks, it is more than two centuries of political and social experimentation with a large democracy.[1] In the context of this national experiment with democracy, our military "social experiment" initially began not in the interest of equality, but because of wartime manpower needs. Detractors used the term then in relation to racial integration.[2] Since the 1970s, the "experiment" in our democracy has been about the All-Volunteer Force, not about women.[3] Secretary Cohen has said that for the 21st century this issue is not about gender or race (or, I would add, sexual orientation) but about national security.

So given the question, "where have we been and where will be in the 21st century?", I would answer as follows. My historical studies show that military women of the past were not really invisible, but they have been largely forgotten. In other words, through the 1940s, 1950s, and 1960s they were in the public view and people knew about them, but they were quickly forgotten. In recent years, as military women have been in the spotlight more, both because of their significant contributions and because of continuing difficulties with integration and acceptance, people have forgotten past contributions and problems.

As a result of this amnesia we continue to engage in numerous and repetitive debates today. "What if women come home from war in body bags?" detractors ask. But military women have come home in body bags since before WWII and there is a memorial now for those who did. Others ask, "what if women become Prisoners of War." That should not be a question. Women have already been captured and held prisoner by our enemies. If female casualties and abuse are real concerns, the question then might be, "what might we do to reduce the number of women ending up in body bags during peace time at home." Perhaps men who say they want to protect women by barring them from service in combat—a largely artificial construct now for the military—should be more concerned with protecting all women in peace time. Perhaps we would give women the tools and training to protect themselves.

This entire debate, all the variations of which we have addressed over and over, is really about cultural reality rather than myth. The question of where military women will be in the 21st century is really up to all of us as citizens. One of the questions we must still answer is, "what constitutes full citizenship in our democracy." How do we judge who is a full citizen? Is it about voting? Is it about paying taxes? Is it about race or gender or color? Is it about religion or sexual orientation? I would submit to you that it is, of course, not about any of these. It is about, perhaps not so obviously, our cultural ideology. In fact for a long time, as you know, citizenship was based on property ownership, gender, and color. So when we initially talked about all men being created equal, we were talking about middle class, white men. And then it became something different gradually and through constitutional amendments. We consciously changed our definition of citizenship. Not because some objective reality about "inalienable rights" and our "creator" changed, but because our ideas about who was actually "endowed" had changed. I think we are generally okay about those changes. But even then, tacitly I would argue, citizenship became based on willingness, or even just liability (conscription), to defend this country—to die and to kill for our ideals. That was coded in the popular imagination as male, and for a time as white. Whereas this was certainly true for citizenship definitions, we need to recognize now that this exclusivity was never so clear cut when it came to military service or dying for this country. In reality, that was never about being only white, or male, or heterosexual.

So the real question for all of us is: "Will we subscribe to a political ideology which we recognize has been transformed for this century and the next as all persons are created equal, and that military necessity demands this?" Because if we are talking about national security, it is not a question of making a choice between military efficiency or equality. Every legitimate study shows that our diversity contributes to our military effectiveness and that equality is compatible with mission accomplishment. The question then is really about who will be classified as full citizens according to our cultural ideology. Whether our cultural ideology will finally match our political ideology or whether we will have to step back from the rhetoric that we have espoused for over 200 years. Will we decide that this is not a debate about women in combat, about women POWs, or about physical standards. It is, as some critics outside the military have proposed, about women not being in the military at all. And if you read those critiques, although their authors may deny it, their ultimate and logical extension is exactly that—an all male military.[4] Because if you are going to include women in the military, and I believe the evidence shows that the nation needs us, then it is about not limiting the contributions we can make to the team. It is not about hurting cohesion or morale or harming efficiency because those are leadership, not gender issues. Where integration works, the leaders believe in it and take care of it and the people follow. Where it does not work, the leaders have abdicated authority and responsibility and have stepped back and allowed people to behave in ways that the people of this country supposedly do not support or believe in.

I believe that the U.S. military is a great institution and my purpose is to help make it better. So in the end the debate moving into the 21st century is about gender, it is about race, it is about sexual orientation. This debate is about the character of our democracy and not about either health/fitness standards or even job performance standards. And the dedication of the women's memorial and its existence in the future, has shown that if what women have are inalienable rights, we have always had them, and if they are about earned rights, we have earned them. Either way, we were here, we are here, and we will be here in the 21st century. We must either embrace the challenges of our democratic experiment or we must abdicate our political ideology.

Notes

1. Defense Secretary William Cohen spoke at the dedication for the Women in Military Service for America Memorial on 18 October 1997. The integration of women in the American military is often referred to pejoratively as a "social experiment" that is detrimental to operational effectiveness, unit cohesiveness (male bonding), and budget efficiencies. See my unpublished dissertation (University of Michigan, 1995) for a discussion of this thesis and comparisons to the same comments about racial integration and the debate about gays in the military.
2. Charles Moskos has written extensively about the differences between racial and gender integration. I disagree with most of his argument.
3. Women were integrated in auxiliary and reserve status before and during World War II. Women were integrated into the services in regular and permanent status by law in 1948.
4. These critics include Elaine Donnelly, Brian Mitchell, Kate O'Bierne, Mona Charen and others.

Chapter 12

So What About the Women?

COL. BARBARA M. LEE[1] *

Since the dawn of the Republic, the Army has been an institution dedicated to the service of our nation. Whether on our own soil or abroad, soldiers have fought and died to uphold our principles and our way of life. Women have always served this nation—sometimes disguised as men and most recently as soldiers in their own right. The increased presence of women in the military has precipitated questions by several special interest groups concerning the legitimacy of their presence. These groups often label women's increased participation as a "social experiment" and feign concern about military readiness.

This paper will posit several ideas concerning why there is an increased presence of women in the Army and briefly touch on several of the current issues of discourse. My comments relate primarily to the Army

*Barbara M. Lee is a Colonel in the Army. She works in the Office of the Secretary of the Army on issues of women in the Army and personnel manpower issues in general. She is pursuing a doctorate in sociology. She is the mother of two sons and a native Virginian.

because I am more familiar with Army policies and practices than I am with those of our sister services. I reiterate that these are my own ideas and are not an official position of the Army or the office in which I serve.

In my mind the true social experiment began in 1973 with the launching of the all-volunteer force (AVF). Admitting increased numbers of women was a natural effect of the AVF and the 1968 change to Public Law 90-130 that lifted the two percent ceiling on the number of women that could serve. Prior to 1973, the Army had few male volunteers but women had always been volunteers.

The social experiment notion revolves around two important recruitment uncertainties:

(1) Would the Army be able to meet "manpower" requirements? and (2) Would the Army be able to attract quality recruits?[2]

The Army worked very hard to make the AVF successful and to satisfy both the "numbers" and quality issues. But to do so created a dramatic change in the demographic composition of the Army. Prior to 1973, we "drafted" a cross-section of the American male population; however, that was not the same population that volunteered for the Army. African- Americans enlisted in greater numbers than were representative of the overall society and the number of women volunteers more than tripled from previous levels in the Army. Today, African-Americans comprise almost 30 percent of the Army—or about twice their representation in the U.S. population. Young majority men were not (and are not) volunteering

It was the AVF, not the Civil Rights Act or any Equal Opportunity Program, that facilitated the increase in women's participation in the Army. And as more women enlisted and additional military occupational specialities (MOS) were opened to them, Army leaders became concerned that there was a difference in the quality of male and female training. Consequently in 1973, the Army began training males and females together during advanced individual training (AIT). Officer training had been similarly gender-integrated and, in 1975, the service academies admitted their first young women. Today, gender integrated basic combat training is conducted for those MOSs that are open to both men and women with gender segregated training in effect for those jobs that are closed to women (Infantry, Armor, and Field Artillery). While the Army views gender-integrated training as a success story, there remain detractors that keep the debate alive about this method of training management.

Who are these young women that join the Army? Are they radical feminists? Or are they women unhappy about being a woman, as critics of womens military service suggest?

As the military becomes less representative of the population and with fewer citizens personally knowing someone that serves, it is natural to wonder what those who do join are like. There will always be a tendency to think "they are not like me" and this may be especially true of the women that join the Army. Surprisingly, while choosing what may still be considered a non-traditional role, these women were not and are not feminists, let alone radical feminists. Most hail from relatively conservative backgrounds and enter the Army because one of their parents (usually the father) has served and they have grown up around the military, some are married to a current service member, others enter because they seek opportunities for travel, education and training that may not be available to them, and others enter because they want to serve their country. Army women are probably very similar to their civilian counterparts of the same age, educational level, and social strata.

The Army could certainly be labeled as a masculine institution and there have been a number of academic papers that describe the military culture as being one that is characterized by its combat, masculine-warrior paradigm. Certainly, many of the tasks performed and the uniforms worn are not even remotely feminine. But there is no indication that the women entering the Army are unhappy being women. While I'm not sure what behaviors would actually manifest themselves if a woman wasn't happy being a woman, I can only say that Army women are daughters, sisters, wives, and mothers who choose to serve their country. Often that service is hard and requires they relinquish aspects of their personal freedom and personal choice. Yet, women serve and the re-enlistment rate for women is significantly higher than that of their male peers (FY 97: Women: 66% and Men 52.5%).

Many of the critics of women serving in the military cite a "double standard" existing between men and women. It is often implied that women degrade the service by their presence and that they are taking a position that would go to an "able bodied man" if they had not entered the Army. This is further complicated by the state of the economy. When the economy is poor and unemployment is high, males are most readily available and interested in military service; however, when the economy is good and we have low unemployment rates, majority men do not enlist in the Army.

What standards are we talking about? Mental or physical? As previously discussed, one measure of equality concerns scoring in the top three mental categories. Overall, women score higher than the men on this quality measure. Almost all of the Category IV[3] recruits are men. Does this constitute a double standard?

The Army Physical Fitness Test (APFT) is another set of standards that Army personnel must meet. The APFT is what the title implies—a measure of the individual's level of physical fitness. The "PT test" is three events, sit-ups, pushups, and a two mile run. These events were selected in the 1980s because a soldier could prepare (and test) without the need for any special equipment or obstacle course. The PT test is not and was never intended to predict which job a person is able to perform. The PT test (as stated before) is intended to indicate an individual's level of fitness. Additionally, the conduct of physical training is frequently used as a group cohesion activity for a unit. The APFT is AGE and GENDER normed. *That is if you are older your standard for reflecting your individual state of fitness is different based on your age—just as it is different based on gender.* Rarely is there any criticism about the difference in standards due to age, but there are frequent criticisms about the difference in standards due to gender.

Since 1992, the Army has gathered data to ensure that BOTH the age and gender standards reflect an *equivalent amount of effort for an equivalent score to eliminate inequities*. The empirical work was completed and the new APFT standards went into effect October 1, 1998.

Separate from the PT Test and physical fitness standards, each Army MOS has physical requirements that are intended to specify what tasks must be performed to fulfill a given skill level for the particular job. Unfortunately, those physical requirements have not been empirically developed or validated, leaving them unreliable and subject to error. Consequently, the MOS physical standards are not used for screening or establishing soldier eligibility in a particular MOS or career field. Recently, the United Kingdom (UK) launched their new gender free Physical Selection Standards (PSS). These standards are comprised of a set of nine measurements and physical tests that have been designed to assess a recruit's capability of achieving the physical requirement to join a specific arm or service. Each of the UK's arms/services has tailored criteria for entrance. The overall purpose of the PSS is to reduce the recruit attrition rates, but this "screening" may also assist the absorption of women in the UK's Artillery, Engineers and other Combat Support Arms that are now open to women.

In 1989, the Berlin wall came down and led to the "outbreak of peace." There was no longer a need for a large standing Army of warfighters when the Soviet Union was no longer a threat. Although there was a "pause" to execute Desert Shield and Desert Storm, the Army has reduced from 800,000 to about 495,000 in size.

Today, the Army has operational deployments in over 74 locations world-wide. In addition to war fighting, peacekeeping and humanitarian aid are now military missions. For an organization that continues to value "warfighting" over and above military operations other than war, this is a difficult time—how do you train and motivate warriors to conduct peace? Does the military culture begin to value skills other than warfighting? If warfighting is only one thing the Army does, how do women figure in?

Notes

1. Disclaimer: The ideas expressed in this essay are mine and do not represent an official position of the U.S. Army or the office in which I serve.
2. Quality is defined as the top three mental categories and the possession of a high school diploma. In today's Army this is 97% of recruits compared with bout 88% in 1987 and 64% during WWII.
3. The lowest mental category the Army accepts.

Chapter 13

ꕤ

Women in the Navy

LINDA L. HEID*

I have been in the Navy for 14 years. I joined the Navy at 17 as an enlisted air traffic controller, after a few years went on to college on a ROTC scholarship, got my college degree, and came back in to the Navy as an officer and headed off to flight school. After flight school, I spent the next six years in support type squadrons because at that time, the Combat Exclusion Law prohibited women from flying in combat squadrons. The support squadrons were also where many male aviators who had disqualified in their fleet squadrons were sent. So, you can imagine it was a pretty interesting place to be: men with bruised egos and women who were chomping at the bit to be included in fleet squadrons. In 1993, the Combat Exclusion Law was repealed, allowing women to fly in combat squadrons, both off land and off aircraft carriers.

---

*Lieutenant Commander Linda L.Heid is a combat aviator in the Navy. She has completed a deployment on an aircraft carrier and has flown combat missions over Iraq.

It was great for me to join a fleet squadron full of hard-charging, motivated aviators and it was very exciting to finally get to do what I was trained for. The majority of men in the squadron were extremely professional and very supportive of the integration of women aviators. There were some that weren't happy we were there and did make life difficult.

I flew EA-6B "prowlers" in my fleet squadron. The EA-6B is a 4 seat jet that jams enemy radars and can also fire the HARM "High Speed Anti-Radiation Missile" against enemy radars. Part of my squadron tour included a six-month cruise on the aircraft carrier USS Abraham Lincoln over in the Persian Gulf. I flew several missions over Iraq in support of Operation Southern Watch. That six month cruise has been definitely the highlight of my career.

Flying off an aircraft carrier is incredible. A cruise is incredibly hard work. Many days you are working 15-20 hours a day, flying twice a day, manning up a jet on the flight deck in 120-degree weather. The experience was simply incredible and I am very proud to have served my country in that capacity.

Women in the military, especially women Aviators are being misrepresented to the public by many people who aren't even in the military, people such as Elaine Donnelly, President of the Center for Military Readiness. We are portrayed as careerist, extreme feminists, women who only care about advancing their careers, women who want separate standards, and women who don't value family.

I would like to present to you that "I am the reality" and I wouldn't describe myself or any of the women aviators I have been associated with as fitting under any of those misperceptions. Until recently, women military aviators have been a relatively silent voice and have not contradicted the negative labels that have been thrust upon them. The military teaches teamwork and camaraderie and we try to work within our own organization, our military, to solve problems and provide solutions. But I feel it is time to speak out against that small derisive minority that is falsely representing our character and qualifications. Let me suggest to you that the military would not let anyone, man or woman, fly a 50 million dollar airplane if he or she were not qualified. The airplane does not know if you are a man or a women. It doesn't care, and I believe the Navy has the same attitude—they just want the best qualified person in the job.

I want to give you the true perception of whom women military aviators are. We are professionals in the work place, like many of you. Our workplace just happens to be the military. We are women who want to succeed on our own merits and qualifications and we do not want a lesser set of standards just because we are women. We just want an equal playing field. We are women who value family and understand the hard choices that have to be made at times concerning career and family. On a personal note, I am a born again Christian and I look forward to getting married and to having children. The bottom line in all of this is that we are women who want to be represented as we really are.

Chapter 14

As We Turn: Army Women in the 21st Century

Rev. Marie E. deYoung*

My reflections about women in the Army are grounded in personal experiences that occurred during my assignment to mixed-gender units in peacetime. My recent chaplain assignments included ground combat engineer battalions both in the Second and Fourth Infantry Divisions, a ground combat engineer company and the Support Squadron for the Second Armored Cavalry Regiment (a Rapid Deployment Force). By taking these assignments, I participated in the experiment to place women in units from which we were excluded until 1993, when the Department of Defense policies to expand the role of women in the military took effect. I can claim close proximity to all of the consequences wrought

*Rev. Marie E. DeYoung served as a Chaplain in the Army. She is currently Director of the Center for Women in Religion and Society at the college of Our Lady of the Lake in San Antonio, Texas. She is President of Citizen Soldiers to Restore Military Integrity.

by recent experiments and policy changes to effect greater integration of women in the fighting force.

Major General Jeanne Holm's book, *Women in the Military: An Unfinished Revolution* details the many legal rights women earned to guarantee military career status. Many of the cases legitimately destroyed those artificial barriers to women's service imposed by Congress or military leaders whose judgment was rooted in cultural norms rather than the demonstrated needs of the service or capability of the women who sought advancement.

Thus, women earned the right to be electricians, mechanics, truck drivers, and fixed wing and helicopter pilots. Women moved beyond traditional careers from safe jobs as office administrators to logisticians, from laundry service workers to helicopter repairpersons. In my own branch, there are approximately 40 women chaplains who serve on active duty out of 1,200 assigned to various installations.

When public advocates converged to remove all vestiges of unjustifiable gender discrimination in the military, the healthy result has been accommodation and adaptation by leaders and men who serve alongside well-qualified women. The ethical nerve is jarred, however, by the selectivity with which women's advocates demand equal treatment under the law.

For decades, feminists fought to have women included in draft registration programs. A reverse discrimination case, brought by a man, finally decided the issue. In 1981, the Supreme Court ruled in *Goldberg v. Roskter* that Congress had the constitutional authority to exclude women from the military draft.[1] In her account of this case, Major General Holm lamented this case would "allow greater discretion in differentiating on the basis of sex."

Yet, women could not make a meaningful contribution to the Army unless gender differentiated standards are accepted and practiced. The tolerance of highly differentiated requirements for physical fitness and strength is just one unequivocal example of feminists' inconsistent demand for equality under the law. In the case of physical standards, women are content to keep the double and lower standard of fitness because it works to their favor in promotion decisions.

Since the Army adopted gender integration policies at the conclusion of the Vietnam War, women have been admitted to the military academies, to OCS programs, and ROTC. Women have achieved status as aviators, physicians, logisticians, administrators, personnel managers, ordinance officers, and more. Without question, women have the intellectual capacity to compete for any job that requires brainpower, but minimal use of physical strength. We cannot ignore biology, however; women from all branches of service have not achieved physical parity with men by any statistical measure. I believe this fact accounts for the lack of certifiable evidence that women have made significant contributions in occupations and assignments that require physical grit. We have no real life stories to tell of women who have the physical strength to lead men out of an ambush situation, or pull men out of burning track vehicles.

Too often, the blame for women's physical weakness is attributed to a lack of equal opportunity, rather than to the biological differences inherited at birth. If only women were allowed access, the argument goes, then women will prove they are strong enough to be unisex boxing champions, football players, even ground combatants. Women boxers and powder puff football players have spoken to the need for gender-separated sports competitions. I can only address the folly of the "access" argument as it relates to women in the Army.

The lack of female combat heroines is not due to existing combat restrictions, as we are led to believe by women who wish to lift these restrictions. In fact, thousands of positions have been opened to women since the Gulf War ended. But wherever women are placed in physically demanding jobs, two must be assigned to do the task one male could do. For example, women can now serve as combat medics to field artillery battalions. Women combat medics can even be attached to an all-male field artillery company. To accommodate this affirmative action, the standards of competence were lowered. Whereas it takes only two men to carry a litter with a wounded soldier, four women are required to do the job.

We simply cannot ignore basic physiology. The evidence is superabundant. As Lieutenant Colonel Gregor testified before the Presidential Commission on the Assignment of Women in the Armed Forces:

(A) Using the standard Army Physical Fitness Test, the upper quintile of women at West Point achieved scores on the test equivalent to the bottom quintile of men.

(B) From these data, he concluded that if the Army selected those who met a nominal standard on the test, 80 percent of the women who applied could not get an Army commission.

(C) Only 21 out of the initial 623 (3.4 percent) achieved a score equal to the male mean score of 260 points.
(D) On the push-up test, only seven percent of women can meet a score of 60, while 78 percent of men exceed it.
(E) Adopting a male standard of fitness at West Point would mean 70 percent of the women he studied would be separated as failures at the end of their junior year, only three percent would be eligible for the Recondo badge, and not one would receive the Army Physical Fitness Badge, because not a single woman achieved a score equal to what men must meet to get the badge.[2]

The Army persists in maintaining dual fitness standards to achieve affirmative action goals for women. At the same time, the Army is engaged in a duplicitous strategy to quell the publicly expressed resentment against the inequities. Especially disappointing: the collusion by the media in creating a false perception that the Army will remedy the discrepancies in any meaningful way. Civilian and military newspapers run headlines suggesting that standards will be equalized, and that overall men and women will have more demanding standards to meet. Mr. Cohen, Secretary of Defense suggested in recent media interviews that physical training standards would be toughened. The cover story from the November 3, 1997 *Army Times* perpetuates the myth of equal treatment, but the text of the article reveals the unmitigated preferential treatment given to women. The new "more fair" standards hold men and women to an equal standard for one event, the Sit-up. Studies have repeatedly shown that women are physiologically equipped to do more sit-ups than men are. In all other categories, women are given extraordinary handicaps.

The fitness differential also persists as the age category advances. As officers and senior non-commissioned officers age, they move away from physically demanding work requirements, such as 12 mile road marches for infantry lieutenants and enlisted soldiers, or the setting up of large tents. Also, senior leaders move to administrative positions. They become staff officers, but can still command respect from junior troops, however, by continuing to excel within their age group. The knowledge that at one time or another, the senior sergeant or officer did all of the physically grueling tasks required of junior soldiers goes a long way in building trust and rapport between junior soldiers and their leaders. On the other hand, credibility evaporates when a leader claims hardships that were never endured.

Shouldn't feminists make serious demands for equal fitness standards for men and women, to preclude any accusations of favoritism, tokenism, or outright insanity in the experimental policies to place women in rugged assignments? Yes, we should, but women's advocates have been conspicuously mute about the double standard. Indeed, any man who raised the question of inferior physical ability, or at least lowered standards for women, is immediately accused of sexual harassment, discrimination, or simply ignorance of the true meaning of equality. As one female Army sergeant explained this new definition of equality to Senator Kempthorne's Armed Services Committee during a hearing in the summer of 1997, "there's equality in the different physical training standards. They're different, not unequal. Women put in equal effort as men, and they are graded on their effort, not the output."

For those unfamiliar with military culture, in the Army, a smidgen of respect can be earned through sincere effort. Professional respect, however, is earned by living up to the core values: courage, competence, and commitment. Professional respect erodes like the soil on the plains of Kansas whenever women distort or exaggerate their potential or real accomplishments in misguided public relations efforts to extort preferential treatment for women. No one has addressed the moral bankruptcy of claiming that equal effort is the same as equal accomplishment. If we were to generalize the rule that soldiers should be rewarded or promoted for effort rather than for competence or accomplishment, the American public would suffer unnecessary losses in combat. The mothers of our combat casualties would surely not find comfort at memorial services for their sons and daughters on hearing the recurring mantra: "We didn't win the battle, but we sure did our best!"

The Army's four foundational values (courage, competence, candor, and commitment) undergird the demands for an honest accounting of women's physical performance in the Army. These values, and not gender bias, are at the heart and root of legitimate complaints about the double standards. Women should not be exempt from scrutiny against these values to achieve a vacuous statistical goal. If women are not physically competent, how can they contribute to the ground combat mission? If they are not willing to abide by the same standards as men, are they demonstrating professional commitment? If the women cannot honestly admit they benefit from the dual standards, and rigidly persist in claiming a right to be evaluated by a lower standard, can they ever expect to be accepted by male peers or respected by men as leaders?

The mid-1980s OCS commissioning standards should prevail Army-wide today. Surely, the pervasive resentment of today's soldiers toward women who flagrantly "get over" by adhering to the lowest possible standards would dissipate if women could be challenged to do their best. Women must prove themselves instead of clinging to their entitled sense of weakness. They must learn to accept their failures, or simply do better, if they wish to win coveted slots. Admission of physically unqualified women places an undue burden on those who are fit—both men and women. In wartime, the physically unfit are not only burdensome—they become dangerous to the mission.

The failures of the first three women who enrolled, but later dropped out of the Citadel can all be attributed to lack of physical ability. Faulkner, the first woman to win admittance as a result of litigation, entered the Citadel grossly overweight, and barely able to meet the minimum Army standards for a woman her age. Faulkner, to her credit, had the intelligence to quit a few days after her entrance to the program. She was surely manipulated and used as a test case by her attorneys and advocates to shatter the glass ceiling at the Citadel, but her "supporters" took no actions, offered no remedial preparation to ensure her competence, and thereby success in completing this rigorous military program. In 1996, four more women entered the Citadel. Two were well qualified to survive the rigorous training, and two were not. The women who dropped out in the fall of 1996 could not march due to pelvic stress fractures, a common ailment in women trainees who are not physically built to carry heavy loads, or to endure the stress of marching. Sadly, the pleas of the two women who dropped out were ignored until the women alleged sexual harassment, a fact that only surfaced through the media when ABC's *20/20* interviewed their two successful female roommates at the conclusion of the first college year.

Experts and women's advocates both agree that one fair solution to the unequal standards in "gender-norming" is to have unisex strength standards that are directly related to military occupational specialties. Often, the argument is made that men and women should not be held to the same generic standard of fitness, but rather, to an equal standard that is job-based. Although this approach would benefit women who are not in physically demanding military occupations, the data overwhelmingly suggests that this change would not level the playing field for women in near combat assignments. The Air Force is the only branch to grade physical fitness according to the needs of a particular job. Their objective data suggests the reason why the other branches of service dare not maintain unisex strength standards. A study of test data for 32,000 Air Force personnel indicated that all men and women were able to meet the minimum lifting requirement of 40 pounds, but sixty-eight percent of men, and only .8 percent of women were capable of meeting the 110-pound lift requirement. Yes, eight-tenths of one percent were capable of meeting the 110-pound lift requirement.[3]

Surely, one does not have to be a sports medicine physician to recognize that more often than not, women are mismatched when they are assigned to physically demanding units. Few women have the strength to be assigned to units where they will have to routinely carry 75-pound rucksacks, lift 100-pound wheels, or carry heavy soldiers from armored units or from their tanks to an ambulance. Yet, women in congress, such as Senator Olympia Snowe, and civilian advocates such as Nancy Duff Campbell, who formed the National Women's Law Center, articulated strong opposition to equal physical fitness standards of any kind.

*****

The impact of pregnancy on military readiness is also of great concern. By planning pregnancies during military schools, women are exempt from all competitive physical training requirements, a feat no man is permitted to accomplish without detriment to his career. One woman officer, a mother of four, never served in a rapid deployment force. After sixteen years of service as a helicopter pilot, she never served in Korea or at other remote hardship assignments, as male pilots are required to do. Men, of course, harbor resentment against women officers who were making rank, "meeting gates," and taking key promotion assignments, when these same women were not required to take their fair share of hardship assignments or compete fairly at schools required for advancement and promotion. Are their complaints unreasonable?

Accommodating pregnant women pilots and support workers is an expensive proposition no matter how the individual woman chooses to resolve her career dilemma. In the recent case of Lieutenant Emma Cuevas, the West Point graduate who asked to be released from active duty to nurse her baby, the taxpayers and the lieutenant's Army peers paid a steep price to accommodate her gender-specific limitations, brought about by a self-imposed medical condition. Cuevas' education cost the American taxpayer one-half million dollars. After completing training for the Blackhawk helicopter, she became pregnant, thus losing her flight status for one year. The Army has a critical shortage of Blackhawk pilots, because of the strenuous deployment cycles. Other pilots covered Cuevas' duties during and after her pregnancy.

When Cuevas returned to active duty, she chose to nurse her baby. Although her commander made special scheduling accommodations to permit the lieutenant to go home to nurse her baby several times per day, she did not feel the Army was caring for her needs adequately. She attempted to resign her commission. The Army refused to accept her resignation, citing the critical shortage of Blackhawk pilots as their legal reason for denying the requested discharge.

A legal battle and a media war ensued. During the legal battle, her attorney stated "Cuevas' superiors allowed her considerable time away from duty and relieved her of flying responsibilities."[4] Cuevas was given an Article 15 (disciplinary action) only after she refused to report for work, citing her decision to stay home and care for her child.[5] Sympathetic television producers and columnists underplayed the Army's extraordinary efforts to work around the gender-specific physical limitations imposed by Cuevas' pregnancy and subsequent choice to nurse her child. Fortunately, the courts were not swayed to grant the lieutenant a legal precedent to breach her contract without legal consequences.

Cuevas left the military and cheated the taxpayers of one-half million dollars of wasted training. One-half million dollars could put 50 young women through four years of a state or city college program. Did the taxpayer get a fair return for their investment in the right of a woman to have it both ways: to receive full training and then not to fulfill her training obligation? Of course not. But neither did the taxpayer get a modest return on their investment in the woman pilot who raised her family at taxpayer expense.

The Army is training women to be pilots who lose years of flight time due to their pregnancies. Pregnant women pilots are grounded and in a non-deployable status for more than one year per pregnancy. Men take a greater proportion of deployments, hardship assignments, and field duty assignments to compensate for this gender-based disability. In a downsizing Army, wouldn't the taxpayer achieve extraordinary savings by paying bonuses to men who could fly during their spouses' childbearing years? Instead, we pay women bonuses and full compensation not to fly or deploy at all.

Without question, soldier pregnancy impacts mission readiness. This is the taboo statement, which stops careers in the swampy Louisiana waters if uttered definitively within earshot of the wrong person. When I was assigned to the Second Armored Cavalry Regiment, Colonel Molino, the 67th Colonel of the Regiment asked a female major to write a paper about the impact of pregnancy on military readiness. The major publicly declined, stating emphatically, "Sir, not until I retire!" Later that month, Colonel Molino, the woman major, and I sat around a lunch table in an Expando Van during a major field exercise. The squadron's female mess sergeant left the field early to take care of her sick baby. As a single mother, she had borne five children out of wedlock, by many different fathers. The mess section was affected not only by the sergeant's single parent responsibilities, though; twelve of the fifteen other women assigned to the dining facility were pregnant. The two non-parent women soldiers in the mess section were so disgusted with this permanent problem that they volunteered for every deployment and hardship assignment from Johnson Island to Cuba to get away from our squadron.

By the spring of 1994, our squadron had 22 percent women assigned. In the mess section, twelve of the fifteen women were pregnant. These women were not only exempt from field duty, they were exempt from their basic duties as cooks, because they could not lift the pots, the supplies, and the equipment required to cook for thousands of soldiers per meal period. On any given day during a deployment training cycle, 35 or 40 women from the squadron were non-deployable due to pregnancy.

When women soldiers are assigned to units that have rugged field duty, the pregnancy rates skyrocket. As the 3rd Infantry Division recently prepared for deployment to Saudi Arabia, battalions reported 9 percent non-deployable soldiers due to pregnancy. When I served combat engineer battalions at Fort Hood, the women became pregnant to get out of the barracks, as well as to get out of field and deployment rotations. In both battalions, the pregnancy rate was more than 50 percent. Senior ranking women officers at Fort Hood complained bitterly to their chaplains about the detrimental impact of pregnancy on unit readiness, but they dared not go on record with their observations. The unwillingness of senior women officers to confront the problem of soldier pregnancy in deploying units makes no sense to professional soldiers, that is to men and women who put the mission and their professional responsibilities above personal gain.

Combine all of the issues that speak to women's performance in this paper: High rates of injury; extremely inferior standards of physical fitness; high rates of non-deployability due to pregnancy; an annual pregnancy rate of 11.9 percent in the Army; the fact that 12.5 percent of women on active duty are single parents; and the first term attrition rate was 37 percent for graduates of the first three years of mixed-gender basic training. When we total these factors, how can we possibly argue that women, as a class of soldiers, as a class of soldiers granted extraordinarily preferential treatment to achieve Affirmative Action goals, are the *sine qua non* to military readiness?

In asking these questions, of course, it is important to expand the questions beyond mere efficacy to the moral consequences of shifting military culture from that of an ethos that rewards responsibility, to an ethos that quibbles over rights and entitlements. We must question the validity of certain legal rights and entitlements gained by women soldiers at the expense of the rights or well being of others. We need to have a public conversation about the moral dimensions of public policies that produce disastrous social consequences when individual rights are absolutized to the exclusion of community or family wholeness.

The most grievous failure of feminists to uphold the constitutional requirement to treat men and women equally under the law can be seen in the plethora of sexual misconduct cases that were publicized by women's advocates to gain "position power" and unearned promotions for women. In almost every case, the litigation, criminal accusations, and public advocacy involved victory of personal rights for a few women over the needs of the military, unit cohesion, or the well being of the individuals affected by sexual relationships outside the traditional norm of marriage.

The legal strategies to win sexual harassment and rape cases have been achieved by depriving male defendants of due process, or equal protection under the law.

For example, male defendants throughout the Army were prevented by rape shield laws from accumulating evidence pertaining to the motivations of their accusers, or evidence that could outright exonerate them as long as the scandal at the Aberdeen Proving Ground brewed. The accused men from Aberdeen had their faces plastered on nightly news, but the Aberdeen women were protected from public scrutiny by "rape shield" laws. Unidentified women made horrendous allegations, but because the women were shielded, persons knowledgeable about the case or the accuser were prevented from contributing knowledge in support of the defendants.

The Army, in its desperation to appease public advocates, who relentlessly accused the military of covering up sexual misconduct, intentionally exploited the rape shield laws to deprive the defendants of information that could easily exonerate them. The media colluded by refusing to report information they had that would properly discredit false accusers. Thus, the government was intentional in depriving men of their right to due process.

In addition, in the Delmar-Simpson trial at Aberdeen Proving Ground, the prosecutors borrowed "constructive rape" theories from feminist legal doctrine, to argue that his accuser and the other women could not give legal consent to have sex with Simpson, despite their participation in multiple sexual encounters with him. According to "constructive rape" theory, because Simpson supervised and outranked his accuser, it was impossible for her to consent. When she sneaked into the back of Simpson's vehicle to have sex at his home, she was being coerced. When she paraded in front of him in diaphanous nighties, she was being coerced. When she bragged to her friends that she finally had sex with Simpson, she must have been in a trance, because indeed, the acts about which she bragged could not have been consensual.

In fact, "constructive rape" theory deprives women of any moral agency for their choices to participate in illicit sex—with the boss, with a married man, with multiple partners, or with someone in senior rank. If "constructive rape" theory is incontrovertible, doesn't it prove beyond a shadow of a doubt the moral inferiority, the moral cowardice of women, and therefore, the danger of letting women serve anywhere in the active duty military? No male soldier, regardless of rank, race, or history of victimization can be legally excused from participating in any peace or war crime because a senior ranking person ordered or encouraged him to participate in the crime.[6] Why should women be held to a lesser standard, yet retained on active duty?

The *Simpson v. United States Army* case may appear a triumph to Nancy Duff Campbell and her co-activists from the Women's National Law Center, because the duplicitous legal strategies saved the careers of 20 or so female participants in the Aberdeen Scandal. This short-term victory for the feminist movement is indisputable. The long-term implications of "constructive rape" theories, however, will prove disastrous to women. The tactics used at Aberdeen Proving Grounds to convict Simpson of rape will ultimately result in more war crimes if the decision is allowed to stand on appeal.

Feminists have unwittingly sanctioned participation in organized acts of war time rape, genocide, and mutilation by subscribing to the dubious theory that women are not free to make moral choices when their superiors invite or demand participation in criminal acts. Therefore, if the "constructive rape" doctrines prevail in the military, the dubious effect will be the justification of illegal behaviors by junior ranking male soldiers, when in the past, we demanded moral courage of all soldiers to resist criminality. I can't help but think that women on the whole, would be better off if the myth of "constructive rape" is debunked, and women held accountable for their own participation in illegal activities such as consensual sex with supervisors.

When the Aberdeen Scandals erupted, the public finally questioned whether the recent mixed-gender training and billeting policies contributed to the never-ending series of sexual misconduct stories that surfaced on Army training posts throughout the world. In 1992, the Army ended separate gender basic training and separate gender sleeping arrangements, both in garrison and in field conditions. These unfortunate changes were undertaken to appease women's advocates, who argued that gender integration would be accomplished more successfully if men and women trained and slept together in all circumstances. Feminists appropriated arguments from the Civil Rights Movement: "Separate is Inherently Unequal," to assert that women's physical ability would improve, that sexual harassment would decrease, and that women would assume more hardcore male assignments with greater ease if men and women trained and slept together in all military environments.

On the face of it, it is hard to fathom how sleeping in mixed gender tents in the field could improve physical fitness scores, or physical stamina in the workplace. The evidence now suggests, moreover, that mixed-gender basic training and mixed-gender sleeping arrangements do little to reduce episodes of sexual harassment and sexual misconduct. Despite the investment of training and personnel dollars in the most expensive and labor-intensive misconduct prevention programs in America, the Army experienced astronomically high numbers of in-discipline sexual harassment and sexual misconduct after mixed-gender policies were adopted.

We should not be surprised that sexual chemistry could produce such negative side effects as illicit sexual activity and sexual harassment when men and women are tented, bunked, or paired up during their basic training experience. The mind is baffled, however, that anyone would continue to push for mixed-gender training and mixed-gender sleeping arrangements after the Kassenbaum-Baker Panel asserted unequivocally that the end results of mixed-gender experiments is of such negative import that women ought to be segregated from men in platoons and smaller units.

Why, when women experience such high rates of failure in mixed-gender training units, is it considered anti-feminist, or anti-woman to advocate for a return to policies that effected higher success statistics for women? Perhaps, because the voice crying from the wilderness has largely come from America's conservative political constituencies. Conservative policy is equated with regressive policy. Hence, the blindness to the failures of gender-integrated training units.

Wouldn't it make more sense to carefully put women in situations where they can succeed based on their merits, rather than place them in circumstance after circumstance that only weakens their concentration, focus, and emotional fortitude to competently complete their training with integrity?

As we turn the century, there is no question that women will continue to participate in active duty military service. There is no question that well-qualified women will continue to make significant and lasting contributions as combat support and combat service support Army staff. The high achievers will continue to approach military service with their focus on duty and responsibility, not waging endless battles for rights and entitlements. There are women who have "made rank" as soldiers, not as symbols for a misbegotten cause. A handful of women generals have served the Army with distinction as military policewomen, adjutants, nurses, and more.

But if women are to achieve greater success in the military, much more will be required of those who believe they deserve greater opportunities to serve. Women will have to submit to the same standards of excellence and performance as men. Women must compete based on merit, not on personal aspirations for glory. Women will have to relate to their brothers-in-arms as women capable of negotiating their problems, disagreements, and disappointments face-to-face, not through high stakes sexual harassment attorneys, media press conferences, or the bully pulpits of congressional women officeholders. The entire thrust of our efforts must shift from the pursuit of entitlements to the gift of service and selflessness. Great women soldiers and officers understand and live these secrets to success. We must find a way to impart these truths to the next generation of women soldiers if women are to have a significant role to play in the Army at the turn of the century.

Notes

1. *Women in the Military: An Unfinished Revolution*, Revised Edition by Major General Jeanne Holm, USAF (Ret.), (Presidio Press: Novato, CA, 1992) pp. 377-78.
2. *Report to the President: Women in Combat*, The Presidential Commission on Assignment of Women in the Armed Forces, (Brassey's: New York, 1993) pp. C-41, C-42.
3. *Women in Combat* . . . , p. C-74, 2.2.3.
4. *Army Times*, 58th year, No. 13, October 27, 1997, p. 8.
5. *Ibid*. P. 8.
6. "Laws of War" Department of the Army Pamphlet 27-1, 27-161-2, 27-10. All soldiers are required to report illegal orders or plans for criminal activity to one of several military authorities: Mps, JAG, IG, Chaplain, higher command headquarters, adjacent headquarters, etc. Soldiers are regularly trained about the distinctions between legal and illegal, unethical or immoral orders.

Part IV

Women in Professional Life

This last section includes the comments of seven successful women in various professions, each of whom has a different story to tell and yet, at the same time, share a fairly common experience. Two lawyers, one academic, one doctor, one nurse, and two journalists relate their similar experience of breaking into a profession which has traditionally been reserved for men.

First, Anne Kimball and Judith Garrett offer strikingly different accounts of their work lives and experiences as women in the practice of law, Kimball as a partner in a major Chicago law firm and Garrett at the Bureau of Prisons at the Department of Justice.

Rita Simon relates her experiences as a young woman entering the halls of academe, interviewing for faculty appointments and interacting with colleagues and their spouses. Her experiences over the course of 40-plus years at universities are not unlike those of the other six women in this section who readily confronted and overcame the challenges of professional life.

Next, Dr. Ilse Lewy recounts the history of women in the medical profession and the strong opposition these women faced. As part of her own history as a young doctor in the 1950s, Dr. Lewy tells of the limited fields in which a woman doctor could practice, the difficulties of raising a family while being on call 24 hours a day, seven days a week, and generally the challenges of combining a full professional life with the domestic role of mother and wife.

Elizabeth Carey covers the same time span and describes her experiences as a hospital nurse and especially the relationship between doctors and nurses. She provides a detailed account of the wide range of day to day activities nurses were called upon to carry out and the lack of respect nurses received from most of the doctors with whom they worked.

Mary Lou Forbes, who began her career in journalism over 54 years ago, remembers the time when women were not involved in the news business in any capacity outside of "soft news," or the society pages. Ms. Forbes nevertheless became a serious journalist, reported on the "hard news," and won a Pulitzer Prize for her efforts in 1959. Similarly, Laurie Goodstein, who is currently a reporter for *The New York Times*, explains her appreciation for the barriers overcome by women in journalism 50 years ago, and notes the complexities and opportunities available to women today as a result. Each of these women recognize, just as the women in other professions did, that the progress made by women in professions formerly dominated by men is unmistakable, meaningful, and irreversible. And for that reason, every professional woman can appreciate the experiences of the past and feel secure in her role for the future.

Chapter 15

ﾑ

Women Partners in Large Law Firms

Anne Kimball*

My perspective of the legal profession is a fairly narrow one. Lawyers do many different things in life. They run companies, they're in Congress, they do lots of different things. My perspective is of a trial lawyer and I have been with the same law firm now for almost 25 years. I have been in private practice the entire time.

I have in my legal career, three significant data points. One is 1959, the year I graduated from college; one is 1972, when I entered law school; and the other is today. I'll begin with 1959. In 1959, I graduated from Smith College. I have to tell you that, at that time, practicing law was not on my radar screen. You know it's hard to figure out why. It was largely a cultural thing, a familial thing. Certainly, Smith College in 1959 did not groom women to practice law. Most people who graduated from Smith College went on to marry and to have children almost

*Anne Kimball is a partner in Wildman, Harrold, Allen & Dixon. She has been with her law firm for over 25 years.

immediately. While some did enter the professions, the majority I dare say did not. My goal in 1959 was to become an academic and that was to me, at that time, a culturally acceptable thing to do—to go on and become a professor of English.

I was also the daughter of a lawyer and the picture my father gave me during the 1950s growing up in New York of the legal profession for women was not particularly appealing. There were very few women. The women there were not well liked by their colleagues. This was through my father's eyes, and it was not a profession where women could succeed to any degree. And in fact, the kind of law firm that he was in, a big Wall Street law firm, had very few women. They were run by and ruled by white men so it's no wonder that the profession did not have an appeal to many of us. There were of course women in the 1959 period who were going to law school and went on to become great lawyers. There's Sandra Day O'Connor and Ruth Bader Ginsberg, but they were the distinct minority. The percentage of women in law school at that time was somewhere between one and three percent.

My father did give me some good advice though in 1959, which was read the "Wall Street Journal" and the "New York Times" every day and always shake hands! And those have continued to be excellent pieces of advice for me and they are pieces that I give to all the young associates, male or female, who work with me. Between 1959 and 1972 I acquired a masters degree, was on my way to getting a Ph.D. in English, and was married, and had four children. And I have to tell you that the reason I went into law was not so much a desire to be a lawyer but there just weren't jobs for professors of English in 1972. It was clear that I was not going to get a tenured position with a PH.D. in English, which is what I wanted, at a university such as the University of Chicago where we were in 1972.

So I decided to go to law school and I went over and applied at the University of Chicago. Two anecdotes: One, I called my father who was still practicing with his Wall Street law firm and I said, "Well, I'm thinking of applying to the University of Chicago Law School and going to law school." He had three things to say to me. One, "you won't get in;" two, "you'll never get a job;" and three, "if you get a job, you will never become a partner in a major law firm." Despite that advice, or maybe because of it, I did walk across the street to the University of Chicago Law School admissions office, plunked myself down and said "I want to go to your law school." They said, "Oh, but you have all those children." I said, "well, I think that's my problem, not your problem." At any rate, I was accepted and embarked on really one of the most exciting periods of my life and what has turned out to be a wonderful and exciting career.

I really enjoyed law school and there was a great family joke about it—compared to raising four children, law school was a snap. But I don't think that that was the case. I really enjoyed the process of a legal education. I enjoyed the Socratic method and the Socratic method is, as some of you may know, under a lot of criticism in the feminists circles today. The Socratic method is basically being asked questions and learning through being asked questions and responding. That certainly was the method of instruction at the University of Chicago Law school. And, in fact, it's the method of instruction I believe in life. You get asked questions about things you say and to the extent you give the right answers or good answers or thoughtful answers, you succeed. And I have found the Socratic method has groomed me to do any number of things, even beyond appearing in a court of law—for example, appearing before large audiences and being able to answer questions from people in large audiences, because of the Socratic method you really have to prepare. You have to think, what question am I going to be asked?

When I'm working with our associates at our law firm, I often ask "what is the hardest question we could be asked about this issue?" That's what we have to answer. That's what we have to be prepared to answer. So I think the Socratic method is a wonderful method of teaching and it is a good method for women as well as men. It is being criticized in some feminist circles today because it is viewed as being tough on women or unfair to women. I think when the method is used properly that's nonsense.

Fifteen percent of my class at the University of Chicago were women. I was the only mother of four in my class, I can promise you. Although my class did have a number of older people in it. Vietnam veterans were in the class. Starr Lynd, the Yale radical, was also in my class and so it was a very diverse and interesting group.

After law school, contrary to my father's prediction, I did get a job with the law firm that I'm at now. Although my law firm had a few women then, it certainly was managed by men. I was the second woman to be hired. When I was interviewed there and came home to my family and sat down at the dinner table and they said, "Well what was your interview like Mom?" I told them it was sort of like a men's gymnasium.

There are a lot of guys snapping towels at each other, verbally of course, and it was a very competitive sport, but I thought I could survive there.

And that's indeed what has happened and I have thrived there. Even though initially when I came it was not a place where people brought their kids or there were many women. But I was given opportunities. And that's what we're talking about today, I think, and certainly my progress from 1959 to 1972 has enormously enlarged my opportunities in life. I have practiced at the firm for almost 25 years. And let me tell you a little bit about what I see today in changes.

In the 1970's, when you went into the courtroom there were not many women there. Nowadays when you go to court it can be a day when there are only women in the courtroom. There are lots of women in the courtroom. There are lots of women trial lawyers. Now there are lots of women judges and that certainly is a huge change. At our law firm we now have a critical mass of women. There are lots of women, particularly in the associate ranks, and they are leading pretty balanced lives. There was a period of time at our firm where the associates I think, were afraid to have children, thinking that that somehow would affect them negatively in moving up through the ranks. Now many of our associates have children. It seems to be an accepted part of life at the firm.

There are three things I want to talk about in terms of being a lawyer today. The first I just touched on was the having families and the more balanced lifestyle. And certainly I see this in men as well as women. When I started practice, the guys did not say, "I have to leave at 5:00 today because I'm coaching my daughter's team." That just did not happen. It happens on a regular basis today. The men are going home to their families earlier. They're participating in their family lives much more. Equally, the women are leading more balanced lifestyles.

The second change is that women are a major part of the workforce and it's not just inside a law firm but it's our customers, our clients. There are many women there. The ranks of in-house counsel in major corporations have many, many women in them. Many women choose to go to corporations rather than to law firms because there are some lifestyle advantages to being with a corporation rather than a law firm, particularly during intense child bearing years. So the number of women customers are increasing and that was never the case. The case used to be that the general counsel of corporations were men. They gave business to their golfing buddies, who were also men. That has changed enormously.

Corporations are also requiring that law firms show a commitment to diversity. There's both gender diversity and racial diversity that major corporations like Dupont want to know, how are we progressing on these issues? Who is involved? And they want women and they want Hispanics, blacks, Asian-Americans, as part of a group working for them. So not only is this a desirable thing, but it's part of the economic necessity of running a law firm now. And that's just a huge change.

Diversity in your lawyer group was not viewed as an economic necessity ten years ago, or even five years ago. It's a market place issue and it's very important.

The third thing I see is that there are a lot of women now who are dissatisfied with the legal profession. I do recruiting for our law firm at the University of Chicago and Harvard and other places. I interview and recruit a lot of young women. Many of them are not thrilled with law school. They simply don't like it. It isn't what they thought it was going to be, and once they get into the profession, they find they aren't enjoying it and they're moving elsewhere. And I don't know why this is the case. I think this is also the case with some men but I think it's less of a phenomenon. Partially I think going to law school has been built up by people to be more than it is. It's a lot of hard work, long hours, and it's a real grind sometimes and you have to really like what you're doing. What you're doing has to be a lot of fun in order to put in consistently 14 hour days.

I'm lucky enough to really like what I'm doing, but for people who really don't like the practice of law, it's just not worth it. So I see more women leaving the profession. The issues that I think remain women's issues at law firms are that very few women still are real rainmakers and real economic forces in law firms. And unless you're an economic force in a law firm you have no power. And I think that's just the way it is—even when they're in law firms in significant numbers, women have not yet gotten to the point where they're generating large amounts of business. There aren't many women doing this. That may change. Hopefully it will change. I think the change in in-house counsel to a more diverse group of people will change that issue and for the better. But I don't think we're there yet.

I have found being a woman has been an enormous advantage to me practicing law. Having had a big family taught me to be very well organized and that is just a critical factor and it's also taught me how to relate better with people. Certainly being a parent has taught me how to relate better to people and it's relationships that really determine a lot of the practice of law.

Chapter 16

ຣດ

Lawyers in Government Service

Judith Simon Garrett*

After a very interesting and gratifying three years of law school, from 1987-1990, I spent one year, 1990-1991, clerking for a judge of the United States District Court for the District of Columbia. My co-clerk (who was a man) and I both very much enjoyed working for the judge. There was no difference, based on gender, in the way the judge treated us. We did joke, however, about the fact that when the secretary was out the judge expected me to make the coffee; never my co-clerk! Both my co-clerk and I accepted jobs with the federal government after our clerkship. I do not know why my co-clerk opted to work for the government (he has since changed jobs twice, first going to a large firm and now working as in-house counsel), but my decision was based in large part on my desire to balance a career and a family. A job with the federal government seemed to offer the best possibility of "having it all."

---

*Judith Simon Garrett, a lawyer, is Chief of Congressional Affairs at the Bureau of Prisons in the Department of Justice.

While in law school and immediately following graduation I worked for several large law firms. I took the jobs mostly because it was something that I felt I should do (since working for such firms is viewed as quite prestigious), but quickly realized that this would not be the career path for me. I noticed that many of the women associates did not have children, opting to wait until they made partner (or left the firm), and the women who did have children had great difficulty finding time to spend with their children. While some of the firms proclaimed to be "family friendly," at the end of the day the number of hours billed was tremendously important, and in all cases associates were expected to work substantially more than 40 hours per week to reach an appropriate number of "billables." I knew that I wanted children and that I wanted to spend substantial amounts of time with them. I did not believe it would be possible to have a successful career at a large firm and also raise my children in the manner I desired; I did not want an au pair spending many evening and weekend hours with the children while I worked at the office. Nor did I want to be exhausted (mentally and physically) from the stress of worrying that I wasn't devoting enough time to the firm, or to the children. I think most mothers feel torn at one time or another, between work and family, regardless of their occupation, but I believed the stress would be overwhelming if I were at a large law firm.

My first position with the Bureau of Prisons was formally titled "honors attorney" since I was hired directly from my clerkship, through the Department of Justice's formal recruiting process; I was a GS-12, earning approximately $45,000 per year. At that time, in 1991, the Bureau of Prisons had approximately 20,000 employees, of whom about 50 were lawyers. There were approximately 10 others attorneys hired at the same time I was, but only a handful were assigned to the central office (headquarters) in Washington, with the others assigned to the six regional offices around the country. The Associate General Counsel who interviewed me and made the job offer was male, as was the Associate General Counsel for whom I was assigned to work, as were the General Counsel and his deputy, as was the Director of the Bureau of Prisons along with the great majority of other senior managers. Despite the "male dominated' nature of the agency, and indeed of the profession, being a women has never, in my view, been a factor in any experience I have had at work, positive or negative.

There have been times during my seven years of working for the Bureau that I have felt I was treated badly, given less than the appropriate amount of respect, and indeed even humiliated. (There have also, of course, been times when I was given inordinate amounts of praise and positive recognition!) For example, one afternoon after I had been promoted to a GS-14 (approximately two years after I was hired) I was speaking about a legal issue to the Chief of Correctional Services, the man responsible for establishing policies and procedures regarding custody issues for the entire Bureau. This man was a GS-15 (the highest grade in the Bureau not counting the Senior Executive Service positions that are reserved for the most senior managers, had worked for the Bureau for at least 15 years having begun as a correctional officer, and was probably nearly 20 years my senior. During the course of our conversation, that was witnessed by three or four of this man's staff (all of whom were GS 14-s) I made a passing reference to the General Counsel and used his first name. The Chief of Correctional Services immediately interrupted me and asked "what grade (civil service rank) are you that you are on a first name basis with the General Counsel?" Nearly all of the attorneys referred to the General Counsel by his first name, at his request.) I was reluctant to disclose my grade because I knew that it would come as a surprise to everyone in the room. While most supervisory staff in the Bureau were aware that lawyers were hired at a relatively high grade (GS-11 or 12, compared to correctional officers who are hired at the GS-5 or GS-6 level) few realized that they could advance to a GS-14 within a couple of years. The staff in the room had earned a GS-14 only after many, many years of service, and I feared they would resent my having achieved the same grade in only a couple of years. The more I resisted disclosing the desired information the more persistent the Chief became, to the point where he became quite belligerent. It was a very uncomfortable situation for all involved. Did it happen because I was a women? I don't think so. It happened because I was a young attorney working for an agency that prides itself on promoting staff from within, staff who began (for the most part) as correctional officers and advanced gradually by working their way through a series of demanding positions. These staff are not terribly receptive to attorneys or other professionals who appear to get a "by," earning the same pay and enjoying the same status as those who have had to prove themselves over the course of many years.

My feeling that being a woman had virtually no impact on my professional experiences with the Bureau of Prisons was validated when there was a change in directorship. In December 1992, the Attorney General appointed Kathleen M. Hawk (now Kathleen Hawk Sawyer as the new Director of the Federal Bureau of Prisons, following the retirement of Director J. Michael Quinlan. I noticed no difference in the treatment of women generally or of myself in particular following the appointment of a woman director. Hiring and promotion decisions appear to be made in similar fashion under both directors, as do other policies and practices. The one interesting change was that the new Director was nearly universally referred to and addressed as "Kathy," while Director Quinlan was most often referred to and certainly addressed as Director Quinlan or Mr. Quinlan.

More than seven years after being hired I am still employed with the Bureau of Prisons and I have no plans to leave. I have advanced and changed positions twice, both at my initiative, and I have found the work challenging and meaningful, the people interesting, and the experience generally very rewarding. Perhaps even more importantly, I have been able to be the primary care giver for nearly one year to an elderly, bed ridden friend, and subsequently to raise two children (one is three years and the other is three months) with no negative effect on my career. During almost my entire tenure with the Bureau I have been tightly constrained in terms of the number of hours and specific hours I could spend at work; this has never been an issue, let alone a problem. I work diligently during the hours I am at work, I eat lunch at my desk while I am reading the mail or other documents, and I spend very little time chatting in the hallway or on the phone. I avoid travel as much as possible (and in fact I have traveled only once in three years. I often respond to voice mail messages on the way to and from work. Aside from a few minutes in the evening that I spend on voice mail, my time at home is my own to spend with the family, uninterrupted by work.

I have certainly made career choices based on my desire to raise children, but I do not feel I have had to make substantial "sacrifices" in terms of my career. Working for the federal government has allowed me to have it all.

Chapter 17

ꕥ

A Look Back at Women in Academia

Rita J. Simon*

Half a lifetime ago, when I was just starting my academic career, the situation of women on university faculties was very different from what it is today. We have come a long way and the changes are almost all for the better. In this brief walk down memory lane I describe the encounters women had when they sought to enter the halls of academe as young faculty, the experiences of those select few who were invited to join the club, the relationships they had with their male colleagues, and the reactions they got from the wives of their colleagues.

But just briefly, let's go back one step earlier to graduate student days. Even during the period when women were almost invisible in the halls of academe, there was a sizeable percentage of women graduate students, especially in the humanities and social sciences. Many of us were awarded various types of university stipends, the most common of

*Rita J. Simon is University Professor in the School of Public Affairs and Washington College of Law at American University. She is President of Women's Freedom Network.

which was an assistantship that involved working with a professor on his research. For women assistants that usually involved typing the professor's papers. A strategy that I developed that served me well in the short run, was to explain to my professor that I did not know how to type (a true statement, I never had a course in typing in high school, and was never motivated to learn on my own) and did not intend to learn. Rather than have me receive a paycheck and do nothing, the professors I worked for found research jobs for me. I ended up doing the same type of work their male assistants did, which usually involved collecting and analyzing data and editing drafts of articles and books. I even got my name on a few publications as a co-author. My memory of many other women assistants was that they were angry, and even bitter, at their second-class treatment.

Let's move on. The dissertation is finished, it has been formally approved and it is time to begin a new life. Letters of inquiry, vitae, reprints, recommendations have all gone out and you are fortunate enough to receive an invitation to visit at a university where you will be considered for a faculty appointment. You come well prepared and your formal talk is well received. Now it is time for that all important interview with the Head or Chair of the Department. By the way, I do not have to worry about which pronouns to use in describing Department Chairs or Professors, because in the former category they were almost certainly men and even in the latter, the large majority were also men.

Perhaps the most striking fact about the job interviews is how different they were depending on whether the candidate was a man or a woman. At the outset, men were asked about the courses they were prepared to teach and about the research they expected to embark upon. They were told about the amount of teaching they would be expected to do, and about the salary they would be offered. Eventually, these topics would be discussed in the interview with a woman candidate, but only if she came up with the right answers to the questions that were posed initially. In my first job interview I was asked if I was "sincere." When I looked puzzled about what he meant, the Department Head explained that he wanted to know if I was serious about my professional future, i.e., did I think of it as a long term commitment or was I likely to get married and start having babies in the next year or so, which would make me a poor investment.

For a woman candidate who was already married, a good part of the interview was spent discussing her husband's situation. Did he already have a job in the community in which the candidate was applying for a position? If she answered that her husband was looking for a job at the same time as the candidate, the Chair assumed that the candidate would not be able to accept a position, if offered, until her husband's situation was stabilized. If the husband was already working in the community in which the university was located, a good many questions were asked about how likely it was that the husband would remain at his present job or whether the firm for which he worked tended to move their employees around quite a bit. These questions, and the responses to them, would usually take quite a while. But following those questions, although for a still smaller percentage of the women candidates, would come questions about children. What arrangements was the candidate likely to make for child care? Could she assure the Department Head that her children would not be in the way, that they would not interfere with her responsibilities at the university? Would she be able to carry on research, serve on committees, and meet her classes, and pay proper attention to her students? Only if, and then when, these issues were satisfactorily resolved would the discussion described in the typical interview with a male candidate begin.

Again, it is time to move on with the fortunate few who survived the job search experience and were offered a faculty position. Now that they were members of a faculty, and in the mid-1950's women represented 22 percent of the faculty at universities all over the country, were there differences in the status of men and women professors?

Let's take a few indices: rank, salary, part or full time positions, and tenure. In 1958-59, the distribution by professorial rank and sex looked like this:[1]

	Full Professors	Associate Professors	Assistant Professors	Instructors	All Ranks
Men	90.5	92.8	79.2	69.3	80.9
Women	9.5	8.0	20.8	30.7	19.1

At all ranks, there were many fewer women than men, but especially among the Associate and Full Professors, women represented less than ten percent of the professorate.

As far as salaries were concerned, the median salary of women professors was $7,899 in 1959-60, compared to a median salary of $9,179 for men professors. Among instructors the differential was smaller: $5,161 for men as opposed to $4,855 for women.[2]

What about collegial relations between men and women, particularly those in the same department or school? In the university dining halls and at local restaurants it was a rare sight to see men and women professors having lunch together. During coffee breaks, the sexes were also usually segregated. If a woman faculty member was the sole representative of her sex in the department, then she would often drink coffee alone, or with the secretaries.

Social activities outside the university setting were often complicated because faculty wives who were full-time homemakers had difficulty relating to their husband's female colleagues. "Why aren't they more like us?" was often the question implicitly and sometimes explicitly asked by the faculty wives, many of whom identified themselves as being "in chemistry" or whatever department in which their husband had an appointment. Since for many of the women on the faculty, their current position was their first job at a university, they tended to be young and childless. The wives expected that these women would soon start having children and that, that would bring an end to their unusual behavior. For many, they were right. Married women faculty members whose husbands also taught at the university were perceived as having dual loyalties. They were expected to participate in the social life of their husband's department as guest and hostess as well as in their own department's social activities. They were also expected to engage in the university-wide committee work and voluntary activities that faculty wives traditionally engaged in. When they did not fulfill their roles as faculty wives, they received negative feedback from the women who played the traditional roles with style and competence. Clearly, sisterhood was not a "buzz word" during this era and to the extent that women felt loyalty to their sex, it did not extend to those who engaged in such deviant behavior as opting to teach at a university.

How different is it today and how different is it likely to be in the twenty-first century for women in academia? First of all, women graduate students and females candidates seeking their first position in academia no longer experience the special treatment I described earlier in this introduction. Indeed, they are eagerly sought after as desirable candidates for positions at many of the most prestigious universities in the country. They also serve as positive and important role models to women graduate students. They are elected to the Executive Committees and Officers of Professional Organizations in all academic disciplines.

What follows are some additional indicators of the changed and improved status of women in academia. As you examine the data that follow, think of it as movement in the right direction and not, in most matters, as an achievement of parity with men. In the January/February 1998 issue of the Women's Freedom Network Newsletter, Judith Kleinfeld reported the following changes in women's professional status:[3]

1. In 1994 women obtained more than 40 percent of the professional degrees, up from less than five percent in 1961. And among African-Americans, women received 57 percent of the professional degrees.
2. Women received 38 percent of the doctoral degrees in 1994 compared to ten percent in 1961. They received forty percent of the doctorates in the Biological and Life Sciences as opposed to twelve percent in 1962.

Forty years ago, women represented 22 percent of all faculty and in 1994, they composed 38 percent of all faculty. The ratio of male to female professorial salaries by rank in 1994 looked like this:

RANK	EARNINGS RATIO
Professor	88.5
Associate Professor	93.0
Assistant Professor	93.0
Instructor	96.0

Given the direction of these ratios, it seems clear that by the time women instructors are promoted to full professors in the twenty-first century, they are likely to earn the same salaries as men.

As we turn to the experiences of women in the fields represented at the Fourth Annual Women's Freedom Network Conference, let us keep in mind the progress women in academia have made.

Notes

1. Source: Jessie Bernard, *Academic Women*, University Park, The Pennsylvania State University Press, 1964, p. 189.
2. National Education Association, "Salaries Paid and Salary Practices in Universities, Colleges, and Junior Colleges," Research Report, 1960. (Washington: NEA, 1960). pp. 959-60.
3. Her source was the *National Center for Educational Statistics, Digest of Educational Statistics, 1996.*

Chapter 18

Women Pediatricians in the 1960s

Ilse Lewy*

Let me begin with a little bit of history. There have been women physicians in this country since the middle of the 19th century, but they were few in number. The first woman to be granted the degree of Doctor of Medicine was Elizabeth Blackwell, who received her degree from Geneva Medical School of Western New York, now Hobart College, in 1849. The New England Female Medical College was incorporated in 1856 in Boston. It eventually merged with Boston University with the provision that BU Medical School be open to women on the same basis as men. In 1867, the Women's Medical College of Pennsylvania had 40 students.

Opposition to the admission of women to the medical profession remained strong for many years. In 1859, the Philadelphia County Medical Society passed a resolution that any member who consulted with women doctors should lose his membership. Clinical instruction, in particular, was held to be unsuitable for women. It was said to be indecent for

*Ilse Lewy is a retired Pediatrician.

women to examine patients in the presence of men. When in 1869 women were finally admitted to clinical lectures at the Pennsylvania Hospital in Philadelphia, the *Evening Bulletin* reported that male students expressed their disapproval "with insolent and offensive language." In the same year, an editorial in the *Buffalo Medical Journal* opined: "If I were to plan with malicious hate the greatest curse I could conceive for women and make them as far as possible loathsome and disgusting to men, I would favor the so-called reform which proposes to make doctors of them."

Despite strong opposition from male doctors, women continued to make headway in the medical profession. In 1879, after a long struggle, the Massachusetts Medical Society was opened to women and other state societies followed. In 1891, there were 132 medical schools in the United States with a total of close to 20,000 students; 1,302 of these were women. Yet even in 1919, the percentage of women students in medical schools was only 6 percent. In the period before World War II, the number of women in the medical profession increased steadily, but women still constituted only a small percentage of the total number of physicians. In the 1950s, a few women, such as Virginia Apgar and Helen Tausig, even attained professorial rank on faculties of medical schools. However, the idea of women teaching in medical schools was still not fully accepted. Women physicians had to be particularly outstanding to achieve membership on a medical faculty.

Most college students, too, were less than happy about having women seek entry into the medical profession. Since there was intense competition for admission to medical school, pre-med students resented women classmates and argued that the girls (one still used this term in those days) wanted to go to medical school mainly to find a doctor as a husband. Another related argument was that female students would soon drop out to get married and have children and that a slot in medical school was thus wasted. Of course, female students occasionally did leave medical school to get married, but some male students also dropped out for one reason or another.

Once in medical school, women students were exposed to jokes and derogatory remarks. Anatomy classes were particularly unpleasant, and anatomy then was a subject to which a lot of time was allotted. Students often tried to outdo each other in vulgarity. I did not attend medical school in this country, but American colleagues have told me that female students here were exposed to the same shenanigans.

At the end of medical school, there again was tight competition for the best internships. This process involved an interview and acceptance depended on the attitude of the interviewer, who usually was a male senior physician. Internship is a period of very hard work. It still is so today, but now interns work one night in three while during the fifties when I did my internship one worked one night in two, including weekends. Night work was, of course, in addition to the regular workday of 8 to 5. Needless to say, this type of schedule was not very compatible with any kind of family life.

During the year of the rotating internship, one looked around for a position as resident which is the next stage in training and prepares the physician for a specialty. Residents also worked long hours and every other night. Today it is possible for two physicians to share one residency position and, thus, each of the two has much more free time. Only after completing my residency training could I think of having children, and so I stayed home for three years doing just that.

Women in the 1950s needed not apply for residencies in certain specialties such as surgery or orthopedics. The assumption was that they did not have enough physical stamina and could not stand long enough on their feet performing the long procedures in these fields. Also they were said not to have enough strength to set bones, etc. Urology, too, was out. It was assumed that men would not see a woman physician to have their prostate examined and at that time there was indeed some truth to this. As to obstetrics, women were discouraged to enter this specialty as well. The medical profession, for all practical purposes, had succeeded in abolishing midwives. The accepted view then was that pregnant women wanted a strong father figure at their side during labor.

I had trained in pediatrics, which includes adolescent medicine, and in the 1950s I worked for several years as a college physician in a women's college. This was a pleasant job because one dealt with a basically healthy population, emergencies were rare and one had regular hours. Most office visits were for minor health problems. However, some situations arose that are quite unthinkable today. The college at that time acted in loco parentis. The girls lived in dormitories supervised by an all-knowing house mother and a 10:00 pm curfew was enforced. If a young woman came to the college medical office and was found to be pregnant, the medical staff had to report this fact to the administration of the college and this usually led to her expulsion. In this set-up, there was no right of confidentiality, and of course under these circumstances, no girl ever dared to seek contraceptive advice from the college medical staff.

Later on I was in solo practice in a small New England town. This meant that I was on call 24 hours a day, including weekends. In this town, as in most such small communities, the local hospital and its emergency room, while having excellent nurses, did not have their own medical staff. Thus, when a child was brought to the emergency room, one of the three pediatricians in town had to rush to the hospital to attend to the patient. Similarly, when a problem arose in the delivery room, such as a premature birth or the need for a Caesarian section or when a baby in the newborn nursery was in trouble, the pediatrician was called and had to leave whatever he or she was doing at the moment—whether it was attending a patient in the office or eating dinner with the family.

My day started with a trip to the hospital to see hospitalized patients, then I had office hours well into the afternoon, and finally I did my house calls. On good days it was possible to be home at a reasonable hour and see the children at the dinner table. However, many times work dragged on into the evening. I often promised the children to attend some school activity or other social event but in fact could not get there. Only in the early 1970s did community hospitals begin to hire a full-time staff for their emergency rooms. By that time, too, a significant number of physicians started to form groups or, as in my case, arrange to cover for each other on a regular basis during nights and weekends. Life thus became easier and more predictable and one could plan activities with the family.

Reliable household help was hard to find and keep in a small town where there were no recent immigrants, legal or illegal, who were willing to do house work. Day care centers did not yet exist. I eventually resorted to au pair girls from Europe, but that was a mixed blessing. Some of these girls had their own personal problems which they brought along. Fortunately, my husband had a more flexible work schedule and most of the time he was able to transport the children to their various activities. He also did the grocery shopping, although we often ended up with items I had no use for.

In my early years in private practice, physicians still made house calls. It was interesting and helpful to see people's homes and get an insight into their way of life. However, it was difficult to examine a child on a kitchen table, perhaps with an opinionated grandmother looking over one's shoulder, not to mention worried parents and curious siblings.

Getting to some of these outlying homes at night or in the middle of a New England snowstorm was no small challenge. Today, people have cars and realize that they can bundle up a child and bring it to the doctor's office where examinations can be carried out in a calmer atmosphere.

Perhaps the most important change in the practice of Pediatrics has been the introduction of Medicaid. All of us used to see sick children of indigent families without charging, but these parents often did not bring in their children on a regular basis. Medicaid has put preventive care such as check-ups, growth and development counseling, and routine immunizations within everybody's reach. In earlier years, such care had been at best sporadic.

A few words about the then prevailing attitude toward patients and especially female patients. Any symptom that was not readily identified as part of a clear-cut disease risked being classified as psychosomatic and was not taken very seriously. Women were considered particularly susceptible to such disorders. Today numerous sophisticated tests are available which enable us to arrive at a more accurate diagnosis. For instance, PMS (premenstrual syndrome) is now an accepted syndrome that is taken seriously and considerable research is devoted to it.

All in all, then, I believe that medical care as well as the position of women in the medical profession have made great strides. Some problems will remain and will not easily go away. Women will always face the challenge of how to combine a full professional life with their domestic role as wives and mothers. I know of no formula that can solve this issue, though the changed attitudes toward family life and household duties on the part of men can undoubtedly help a lot.

Chapter 19

ꕤ

Nursing Practice in Hospitals From the 1950s to the 1970s

ELIZABETH T. CAREY*

Forty five years ago I was one of fourteen students, dressed in identical uniforms, who eagerly entered the hospital world to become nurses. There have been many changes in nursing during that time, but in some crucial areas movement was as slow as a snail's pace. The following is a description, and with the advantage of hindsight, an interpretation of my hospital nursing experiences in earlier times.

When I first began to practice nursing in the 50s as a student, then as a graduate Registered Nurse, I worked in a 900 bed hospital in Rhode Island. I was responsible for and coordinated the care of patients and carried out treatments prescribed by the doctor. Also, I had duties not directly related to patient care. I dusted and washed the beds (including the springs) and window sills, watered the flowers and mopped up after the occasional spilled urinal. Cleaning as part of the nurse's duties was

*Elizabeth T. Carey is a retired Registered Nurse and Professor of Nursing.

a holdover from Florence Nightingales' time. Over a hundred years ago, she wrote the first description of what nurses do to promote health: get rid of filth and maintain a clean environment to speed healing and lower the death rate. Nursing duties, in other words, were very broad and what was specifically "nursing" as separate from following doctor's orders and doing chores that could be done more easily and economically by the janitorial staff, provides a clue that changes in nursing were slow in coming. There were clearly prescribed roles for everyone in the hospital except for nurses. For example, one knew what an x-ray technician or a dietitian did, but oddly enough, the nurses' role was and continued to remain poorly defined.

One distinct nursing activity, and the most important part of care, was giving the patient a bed bath, since a large part of healing consisted of many days of bed rest. In those low tech times, medicine relied heavily on the body's natural healing properties believing that rest was curative when augmented by medicinal or surgical intervention. I brought a large tub of hot water to the patient. He washed his face and I washed everything else, including a soothing backrub and foot soak. Patient's backs were washed and rubbed in the afternoon for comfort and again at night to promote restful sleep. I describe the bath because that was a nursing action that had a scientific basis. Nursing then, as now, viewed the patient holistically. The bath was considered therapeutic. It stimulated the restorative powers of the body: rubbing the skin promoted circulation, massage relaxed the body and helped to reduce pain, and the nurse's intimate but professional touch and presence reflected empathetic caring and reassurance. That was what was meant by being a bedside nurse.

Nurses, of course, carried out doctor's orders. I gave injections before the day of plastic disposables, sterilizing syringes and sharpening needles. If the patient needed oxygen, I wheeled a large tank on a hand truck to the bedside and used a wrench to turn it on. When a patient died, I washed the body and wheeled it to the morgue. It is hard to imagine that just 40 years ago nursing and technology was that primitive! There were no "Code Blues" then, and although nurses were very busy and often worked overtime gratis, medical crises were infrequent. Patients had operations, or they received palliative care during long illnesses or died quietly, with the nurse present.

Units or wards were staffed and run by RN's or student nurses; there was an occasional Practical Nurse and one helper, or "go-fer," for 36 patients. The nurses were the only trained staff with the patients 24 hours a day. Anyone who came to the ward, family members, ancillary staff or the doctor was there only briefly. I and my fellow nurses were the main and often only link between the doctors, patient, family and other departments such as x-ray, laboratory and dietary. Part of our day included frequent calls to other hospital departments to arrange services or treatment not done by nursing, reassuring the family or calling the chaplain. It took organizational skill to combine these activities with bedside care, but was largely unacknowledged.

When doctors came to see their patients, nurses adopted a different role. The "provider of continuous care" suddenly became an assistant or handmaiden: doctors ordered and nurses jumped into action interrupting their own schedules, helping the doctor with his examinations or treatments and unquestioningly accepting whatever the doctor ordered. Communication between the doctors and nurses could hardly be described as being on an equal footing: the doctor asked questions that elicited data, and questions by the nurse were only to clarify what was ordered. Nurses' opinions and interpretations of data were devalued or were considered impudent or threatening since nurses were viewed as serving the doctors in a supportive role. There was no collaboration because doctors and nurses did not work cooperatively. The irony was that in a climate of open discussion the nurse could have given better care, since the nurses' educated vigilance and action was indispensable to the patient's optimal recovery. As a result, nurses talked mainly to each other.

When the doctor left, the nurse once again assumed her position of authority regarding the patient's care, using her judgement about the patient's condition, including exercising a great deal of latitude about the dosage and times for giving medications for pain. One can imagine the harm that could occur to the patient if the nurse had not exercised her judgement, but this important piece of what nurses did was beyond the view of others outside the ward and hospital. Interestingly, despite the nurses' responsibilities for maintaining the patient's welfare and involvement with hospital services, the nurse had no communication outside of nursing with higher administrative levels of the hospital regarding patient care. The invisibility of the nurse beyond the ward was part of the hospital structure. More about this later.

I

The evolution of hospitals as curative modern institutions and the formal education of nurses and doctors all occurred about the same time in the early part of the twentieth century, but the effect of nurses' education played a large part in the marginalization and invisibility.

Nursing Education

There were two types of basic education preparation for Registered Nurses in the 50's: a four or five year Baccalaureate in Science and a three year Diploma Program. I chose a university program. I had five semesters of liberal arts and science courses and five semesters at various affiliated hospitals for clinical experience.

There were very new nurses with generic Baccalaureate degrees in those days. Until 1970 approximately 95% of the Registered Nurses (RNs) in the United States graduated from a Diploma Program. Nurses who wanted a Baccalaureate degree after obtaining their Diploma went to college part time while working.

Until the early 1970s, when escalating costs closed nursing schools, almost every hospital in the United States, large or small, created and supported a Diploma program to provide itself with nursing staff. In exchange, students would get clinical experience. The hospital had its schools and dorms in close proximity so that students could come and go to work quickly and safely at all hours. The schools provided several advantages for the hospital:

1. There would be a very inexpensive supply of workers to staff the hospital day and night;
2. Nurses would provide safe care. As late as the 1940s, women could be hired as nurses based on personal experience but without formal training or evidence of competency. By contrast, students who graduated from the hospital's structured training program could quickly and easily assume hospital duties safely and were knowledgeable of the institutions' expectations and customs; and
3. There would be a steady supply of RNs entering the workforce, a constant concern, since during most of the time there were nursing shortages.

Students, primarily female, entered the program right after high school. Many came from the middle class. They were smart and ambitious, postponing marriage and leaving home to get an education. Many later reached high levels in nursing administration and education. A rare few were married or were male.

Diploma education was based on an apprentice system, following Nightingale's model. Students were trained by faculty who were mostly graduates of the same program. There were no university courses because the programs were not designed to provide a liberal or general education; the focus was on the need for practical rather than academic skills. Students learned to subordinate their own needs in the altruistic believe that to do good for others was the greater goal. They were evaluated primarily on three criteria: 1. On conduct: they recognized and acknowledged authority and did not argue; 2. Tidiness; their hair was kept off the collar, the uniform and cap were starched crisp and shoelaces were washed; 3. And skills; they demonstrated the ability to carry out procedures strictly as taught.

University students were similarly evaluated in their hospital practicum but our academic preparation went beyond technical skill. We were expected to have a better scientific understanding and therefore greater ability to recognize when the patient's condition warranted a different nursing approach or a doctor's intervention, and to be able to exercise leadership in ward management.

Classroom education for Diploma students consisted of 3-4 hours of class and practice a day; the rest of the 44 hour week students worked in the hospital. They worked day, evening or night shifts mostly under the supervision of the head nurse. In their third and last year, students were minimally supervised and were in charge of units, working very much like unpaid professionals.

The apprenticeship included rules of discipline and obedience to authority which was instilled by the hospital which financially supported the school where the young women were trained, housed, and fed in exchange for free labor or educational experience. This isolating, practical education produced intensely loyal, highly skilled, narrowly educated nurses who were vulnerable to the authoritarian control of the hospital administration and the domination of the doctors.

Sociocultural influences

There were two major influences from the early part of this century that affected developing hospital institutions. One was the subjugation and servitude of women and their widespread economic exploitation, and secondly, the care of the sick by nurturing women moved from the intimacy of the home to the controlled and distancing environment of the hospital. For hospitals, hierarchal and paternalistic, these forces fit in nicely with their own structure: their nurses could provide a public extension of private domestic labor and selflessly care for the hospital family at low wages, loyal and devoted. They were even rented at a profit to those wanting private care.[1]

Gradually, education for doctors, who were predominantly male, became more formalized and the American Medical Association (AMA) became more powerful. Gender role differences became more fixed and accepted. Attempts to develop and advance nursing by its professional organizations were often blocked by the AMA and the American Hospital Association (AHA) working in tandem. In the 1940's, national nursing organizations appealed to the AHA to allow it to educate and manage its own profession in order to reduce the hospital's influence and control on nursing education and practice, with little effect. Over the years, leaders in the health field, hospital administrators and the AMA committee on nursing maintained its authority over the profession by strongly defending its right to decide the role, education and direction of nursing.[2] This etched in the minds of many that nurses were to be subservient to doctors and to be economically advantageous to hospitals. This pattern of control defined nursing's struggle with exploitation and was the biggest obstacle to clarifying the identity of the profession and promoting collective strength.

II

When I moved to the Midwest, I worked for several years as a staff nurse in three small hospitals in a medium sized community. I also taught Diploma students. Advances in technology over time changed what nurses did, but many things remained the same. Gender and class differences in education, expertise and practice between nurses and doctors was a significant factor in their relationships, but the socialization of the nurse into a patriarchal hospital system perpetuated her sense of inferiority and the status quo. Nurses had no input in policy making, control of budgets or even a say in planning or remodeling the units where they would work. No example could more powerfully indicate the invisibility and voicelessness of the nurse than the opening in the mid 1980s of a new architecturally designed hospital wing, which had lovely rooms, storage and equipment . . . but no nurses' station with a medicine room or a sink!

The Hospital-Doctor-Nurse-Relationship

When I was a staff nurse, I worked with Diploma graduates. Nurses were considered generalists in the hospital and differences in the levels of education, while acknowledged, were ignored. All nurses were considered able to work anywhere—one day obstetrics, the next a medical or surgical unit, or even the Emergency Room.

In those times doctors had a lot of power, prestige, authority and visibility (in contrast to nurses), not only in the hospital but with the public. Doctors in private practice sent their patients to the small hospitals, providing them with their economic life blood. The doctor used hospital services to carry out medical care as if the staff were his employees. He was treated with respect and consideration for *his* busy schedule and needs, so that he would not take his patients elsewhere. The public was awed by the doctor's knowledge and authority and accepted medical paternalism without question. The doctor told the patient what treatment he would get and rarely informed him of his diagnosis, especially if it was cancer.

The positions of status, power and inferiority between the nurses and doctors played out in verbal and sexual harassment. Of course, it wasn't called sexual harassment in those days. It just went with the territory. I have been propositioned, patted, cornered and kissed until I was in my early 40's. An example of this occurred with an MD who came on the unit every day. If I happened to be in the hall, he would approach me and sweep me in his arms and give me a kiss on the cheek. This was met by gales of laughter by any doctors or nurses present. I wasn't the only nurse he approached. He considered it good fun. After several months of this, the doctor, not being an equal opportunity kisser, was accosted by a rather obese nurse who demanded her turn to be kissed. He complied, looking harassed. He never approached the nurses again. Mostly, I handled such situations by either saying I was not interested or I reacted with great annoyance. I did not consider it harassment, not knowing it was that, perhaps because my responses worked. I know other nurses who spent a lot of time hiding to avoid the harasser. We talked about which doctors one had to avoid but it was unthinkable to lodge a complaint we knew would be ineffective.

The most disturbing problem, however, was the large amount of verbal harassment and abuse directed by doctors towards nurses, particularly in the small hospitals. I have been the recipient of and overheard tirades and yelling by doctors regarding my or fellow nurses' supposed incompetence. The fury directed at the nurse sometimes occurred in the presence of patients. Outbursts often related to events from other shifts over which the nurse had no control: lab or x-rays not done, the patient ate when he should have been fasting, anger because phone calls to the doctor were made unnecessarily or should have been made sooner, etc. The nurses' errors in the eyes of the doctors were perceived as stupidity or carelessness. The nurse said very little in her own defense, for she believed he was right. He was a lot more knowledgeable than she, and he was very adroit in letting her know it.

Administrative supports for nurses was minimal and effectively maintained their passivity. If a nurse complained about a doctor, nursing supervisors excused the doctor. If the doctor complained about a nurse, she was chastised. The doctor's power, real or imagined, economic or professional, was a threat. You could be fired. Although the staff knew that nurses were crucial to the institution, the hierarchal lines of authority insured distance and marginalization. As for myself, I went along with the hospital's structure for many years. Finally, I had enough. I began reporting and writing incident reports to administration about doctors who blatantly discriminated against African-Americans, and reported and questioned incompetency. Other nurses had enough too. In 1969, nurses requested a meeting with administration (unheard of at that time) to discuss issues important to them and were, in effect, refused. This was followed by firing a loyal, competent nurse who was considered an agitator and unionizer. The nurses went on strike. Did we win? Alas, no. Local doctors arose as one and gave the hospital administration considerable support.

I have addressed just one type of nursing, the one I knew best. There were and are many areas for nurses to practice outside the oppressive atmosphere of the hospital . Nurses who wanted more autonomy and independence chose to work in clinics or did community nursing, taught, or left the field altogether. I chose the hospital because I liked the curative aspects of health care. It was exciting, there was constant variety and a lot of opportunities to learn. The satisfaction of providing care to patients were often subtle but frequent: a grateful look spoke volumes. In general, ward nurses were supportive of one another, recognized each other's efforts and knew that what was done was vital, and not infrequently, lifesaving.

Hope of the Future

In the late 60s changes were occurring that would help to alter the public's perception about what nurses could do; slowly doctors gave nurses grudging respect and finally, nurses began to find their voice. Four important trends had a large impact on nursing:

1. Nursing education moved out of the hospital into Community Colleges. In a more academic, less paternalistic climate, the apprentice model began to be modified.
2. Although Community colleges did an admirable job preparing technical nurses, more nurses were getting Baccalaureate, Masters, and PhDs, often with federal funds designated for nursing education.
3. Changes within the hospital: Increasing strides in medical research, technology, diagnostics and treatment gave rise to the development of Coronary Care and Intensive Care Units. Nurses took detailed pathophysiology courses in order to work in CCU and ICU's that increased their knowledge, competence, confidence and accountability. It helped them become specialized and clarified their role. These highly skilled nurses were respected by their peers and were less subservient to doctors. Doctors, in turn, were more collegial in this environment.
4. Nurses took matters into their own hands. With unionization the power of solidarity helped break the tight stranglehold of paternalistic bureaucracy. Nurses were invited to participate in organizational meetings, and salaries and fringe benefits became comparable to those in similar professions.

III

For nurses who had chosen a profession traditionally open to women and for whom passivity and submission were clearly defined roles, the social forces both within and outside of the hospital coupled with an institutional apprenticeship taught by people trained in the same hospital effectively insured their continued marginalization and exploitation. For nurses during those times, the belief that personal sacrifice to provide service to those less fortunate was its own reward. The professional intimacy in caring for patients who were bedfast for a week or more was often mutually satisfying: after medical intervention, the nurse had a sense of accomplishment when noting the patient's recovery during her care, and the patient appreciated the ministrations that gave him comfort and helped him progress. Viewed from a distance, such activities seem menial; yet for the individual patient and the family that worried about him, the nurses' availability, action, and relational work reflected caring, and that was personally valued. Those actions, and the knowledge that what nurses do is indispensable to the work of medicine, was not recognized as having substance by the hospitals providing this service, and slowed the development of nursing into a strong profession with status, complementary to, coinciding with, yet distinct from that of physicians.

Notes

1. Ashley, Jo Ann. *Hospitals, Paternalism and the Role of the Nurse*. New York: Columbia Teachers College Press, 1976.
2. Ibid.

Chapter 20

The Woman Journalist

Mary Lou Forbes*

I started in the news business 54 years ago. I was at the University of Maryland during World War II and I'm a University of Maryland dropout. That's my academic credentials, although I have subsequently taught at the Medille School of Journalism and other places such as George Washington University by invitation. You overcome those handicaps like lack of degrees by your career experience. Those of you in the news business know how that is.

I left college at the University of Maryland when I discovered my mother had no money. We didn't have government programs, we didn't have scholarships so I got a job at the end of the bus line to give me enough money to go back to college the next year. I was majoring in mathematics. Can you believe from that I wandered into the news business?

---

*Mary Lou Forbes is Editor of "Commentary" in the *Washington Times*. She is the recipient of a Pulitzer Prize.

At that time, the "Evening Star" was located on Pennsylvania Avenue immediately cross from the AB&W bus line. During World War II you couldn't drive to work. There wasn't any gas and you really had to get there on a bus. I got off the bus and went over to the "Evening Star" and answered an ad for an accountant. They didn't have that job still open but they offered me something called a "copy boy." I had never heard of a copy boy's role but the way the personnel department started describing it to me—that you'd be in the newsroom where the paper is put together and this and that—it sounded like fun. It paid $17 a week! Believe me, it didn't take a month before I forgot math. I can't even keep my checkbook straight any more. I fell in love with the news business and it was the beginning of a love affair that endures to this day. I was with the "Star" 37 years. I went down with the sinking ship. In fact George Beverage and I wrote the last byline—"The obituary" let's call it. And that was the first time that I used the name Mary Lou Forbes. I'd always used Mary Lou Warner, which I'd achieved some recognition with, but by the time the "Star" died I had a son. So motherhood prevailed and the byline went up there—Mary Lou Forbes. By that time my son was seven or eight years old. Yes, I was in the news business 25 years before I had a baby but that's part of the story as I go along.

The news business had not been one that was highly touted as a great career opportunity for women outside of the society pages, the soft news as we would call it. And the excitement that I found in the newsroom convinced me early on that that's where I wanted to stay. I wanted to cover the fires, the politics, and so forth. I wanted to chase the fires. And I must say that men were helpful to me every step of the way. That's why I'm not against the new feminism, but I just don't understand it, because it seems to hate men so. I'm glad there are a few men here to appreciate this. My husband would appreciate it.

Women also were getting help from Eleanor Roosevelt. I was just a beginner at that time and she started having press conferences which she reserved for women only but, there again, the women were being used in a strictly female assignment because she was talking about issues presumably of interest to women and the women were assigned to cover it. This was still segregating women from the hard news coverage that I knew I wanted to pursue by that time.

There were women editors of small town newspapers years ago. Perhaps not the big ones, but small town papers and the big papers would hire these women as stringers and they would cover the little county board meetings, etcetera. A lot of women gained experience in how to cover a story that way. Until the men started coming back and while the men were away, we did start to move into more exciting assignments because there was no choice. There were no men available during World War II unless they were married with lots of children or something else. And ironically, one of the concerns that all of us who marched into the newsroom then shared was that we didn't want the wives to think that we were there pursuing their husbands. The only men in the newsroom were husbands and—so we had you might say our own little sex issue at the time, the opposite of the kind that we hear so much today. Were we discriminated against? I would say spare me that word because whining about discrimination has so distorted its meaning that I think the word has almost become meaningless. It's difficult any longer for me to determine whether real discrimination exists or whether it is being used as a cash count. In fact, with the size of some of these awards, I find myself thinking, "I wonder if the statute of limitations has expired or could I still collect?"

But I put that aside because yes, we did face preconceived notions of what women were equipped to do. But these stereotypes became a challenge to be confronted, disproved and overcome. And the male coworkers who in today's environment are the designated pole cats, they were the most enthusiastic supporters and door openers for every threshold that I crossed. Now there are, of course, some caveats to this. I remember the day that I had done a very good job being a copy girl or boy and I had then become a dictationist taking the big stories like the day Roosevelt died and things like that.

I had worked my way through the ropes and they had an opening for a beginning reporter and I remember the managing editor calling me in and talking to me. "You've done so well, would you like to become a reporter?" The first thing he asked me was, "You're not about to get married are you?" Well, that did scare me—I wasn't holding hands with anyone then but it did sort of scare me out of 15 years of marriage. I didn't marry until a little later than most people and, in fact, if there's any real complaint to look back on I think a lot of women who would have married were afraid they would lose their career or it would interrupt their career path.

I take pride in the fact that maybe I changed that a little bit. By the time I got married, they didn't want me to leave. They wanted to keep me around forever, and they continued to give me good assignments.

It's immodest of me to mention it, but it will look great in my obituary. In 1959, I was fortunate enough to win a Pulitzer Prize. Again, that was under the name of Mary Lou Warner. I think I was the first woman ever to be awarded one and you didn't write big stories saying, "Woman wins Pulitzer Prize." It seemed like it was part of the natural evolution of things, that we were progressing and it would have been embarrassing to say, "Hey, a woman won a Pulitzer Prize." I mean it would just be tacky, really tacky. When I did win one, this was a little embarrassing for the "Star" because they hadn't already made an editor out of me. Now this was another threshold. No woman had been made an editor in the newsroom of a major metropolitan daily. When I was asked if I wanted it, I said yes because, gee whiz, what an honor. I could be the boss, I could tell the other people what to do. The editor of the paper said, "Well, do you think men will do what you ask them to do? Will they take your orders?" And I said, "Yes, because they know I've been a very good reporter." Oh, I'm on an ego trip here but I had been a very good reporter. I would never have to ask anyone to do anything that I hadn't done myself.

So I took the job and was assistant state editor and then state editor and ultimately became city editor of the "Washington Star," which was regarded as a relatively conservative paper. We didn't think about those conservative/liberal things quite so much back then. I was an editor long before the "Washington Post" had a female city editor. I tease the "Post" a little bit on this one. But somehow all of these hurdles were surmounted without benefit of litigation or affirmative action or any other such mechanisms and all, again, with the help of the men who were encouraging you every bit of the way.

After I was made an editor, I later learned from Steve Green, who is now a reporter with the Copley News Bureau here and once worked for me, that every reporter or every job applicant who came to work was asked after I was made an editor, "Do you mind working for a woman?" And so as far as I know none of them ever said yes. So, you see, all these men out there aren't such bad guys after all. They worked for me, they did what I asked them to do.

And I look back on those years not with a feeling that we were held back, but that we were given an opportunity and if you could demonstrate your ability, you could get ahead. That is what I think separates journalism from a lot of other careers where it may not be as easy to demonstrate your competence. But in the news business you're so close to the end product and if you have imagination and good perception for what's news, it's easy to prove your competence. I think it's offered great career opportunities for women and I think it'll continue to do so.

Chapter 21

A Woman Reporter in the '90s

Laurie Goodstein*

When I left my job at the New York office of "The Washington Post" recently, a friend who worked in the library there gave me a book called "Ladies of the Press." It was a tattered old book, published in 1936. She had removed it from the shelf because she'd been given the job, as many news librarians are nowadays, of dumping everything old and rare and valuable from the library shelves—namely books—and replacing them with computer terminals so that we can get access to the same information that everybody else has.

Anyway, I was reading this book before coming here so I'd get a sense of just how far the "Ladies of the Press" have come. Take Sally Joy of Vermont, who at age 18, five years after the Civil War ended, talked her way into a job at the "Boston Post." Her befuddled male co-workers carpeted the floors of the city room with newspaper to prevent her work uniform, a white satin ball gown, from picking up dust. For any assignment that required her to stay out later than 7:00 p.m., they

*Laurie Goodstein is a reporter for the *New York Times*.

sent her out with an escort. But Sally Joy proved that she could write. She was the only woman sent to cover the suffrage convention in Vermont. She won promotions, was given her own society column, made a name for herself . . . and then got married. And so she quit.

Sally Joy's story shows us both how far we have progressed, and at the same time how little things have changed. Let me deal first with the progress. For one thing, women writers are no longer relegated to the women's pages or society columns, as was Sally Joy. You will find women reporters wherever there are male reporters—filing from war zones, investigating City Hall, by lined on the front page. There are women city editors, women publishers, women managing editors. More than half the students in many journalism schools are women. This is not to say that women have achieved complete parity. They have not, and many a journalism study has examined what to do about that. But the great barriers of old have been broken down. So after decades of proving ourselves in the newsroom, the question is no longer whether a woman can rise to the top ranks of our nation's newsrooms. I think the question now is, can you have a career as a news reporter and at the same time have a life? Can you be a consistent partner or wife, can you be a responsible mother, and still beat the competition at breaking news?

In any job, of course it's hard to balance work and family. But it's a particular challenge in the news business. And please understand, I'm talking here about daily news reporters working for daily outlets like newspapers, both because this is the work I know and because it poses particular quandaries. News is unrelenting, and it is unpredictable. Reporters live with the daily uncertainty whether they will make it to the door of the day care center to pick up their children by closing time. When TWA flight 800 recently crashed off Long Island, I left my sleeping son at home with my husband and didn't see them again for three days. When Rabbi Meyer Kahane was assassinated in New York City, I had to excuse myself from my own dinner party. This is not the kind of life that makes for family stability. It's a little bit like being a volunteer fireman. You never know when the alarm is going to sound. And a firestorm of news can burn on for days or even weeks because once a big story breaks, it's not over when you file the first story. The crisis becomes a running story and it may be two or three weeks, maybe a month or far longer before your life gets back to normal.

So, am I saying that daily journalism is incompatible with family life? Am I saying that we all have to be like Sally Joy and quit if we marry? No. It is possible to be both reporter and mother. Many women are doing it, and seem to be excelling at both. But to do it, most of them, like me, need support either at work, or at home, and preferably at both. It requires doing things differently than in the past. And I'm not just talking about feeding the kids frozen dinners. I'm talking about true, institutional change on the part of both co-workers and couples. On the job, for example, more newsrooms are allowing people to work part-time. At The New York Times, where I now work, a number of news reporters, including me, are working four-day weeks. In some other news organizations, reporters are sharing jobs, and so are editors. I am not saying that either of these arrangements is common, and there is often still resistance both justified and unjustified on the part of newsroom management. But it is no longer considered revolutionary.

Family-friendly work arrangements are even beginning to affect what has long been considered the elite corps of news reporting—the foreign correspondents. At some large newspapers, like The New York Times, where I work now, a surprising number of the foreign correspondents are actually husband-and-wife teams. And it's not as though the husband is the senior correspondent, and the wife the junior. In most cases, they are partners equally qualified to cover the big story. If they have children with them overseas, and many do, they take turns staying at home in the capital while their spouse/colleague dashes off to the hinterlands to cover that earthquake or coup d'etat.

On a purely anecdotal basis—and journalism is an enterprise where anecdotes count for something—I am seeing more responsiveness on the part of senior editors to individual requests for flexibility. I know of a very respected editor at The Washington Post who had left journalism to raise her children, and was lured back to work on a rather unorthodox schedule. Now she comes in early, assigns the stories for the day, and leaves by mid-afternoon so that she can be home by the time her children return from school.

I also know a reporter who had a very demanding assignment that frequently kept her out working at nights and on weekends. So she asked and was allowed to take a summer off before her daughter started kindergarten. As far as I know, this woman was not penalized for taking this time off to be with her young child. She returned to work, at a different assignment but with a great career ahead of her. She happens to be part of a team that won a Pulitzer in 1999. But flexibility on the job is not enough. The other necessary ingredient is true teamwork between the parents. My husband, Peter, is one of those rare fathers who, I can honestly say, really does put his family first. He's the one there when the babysitter comes in the morning, because I leave first. He's often the first one home. He takes care of our son Gabriel, who will turn two next week, on the evenings when I have to stay late and the occasional weekends when I am traveling. On other weekends I cover for him while he hunkers down at the computer. I know that his work is important, but he also knows that mine is important, and we try to give each other the time to do it.

Admittedly, we do have several key advantages that make this fortunate life possible: he runs his own business and sets his own hours. And we are blessed with, and can afford, a loving, reliable babysitter. I realize these are luxuries that many families do not have. However, when both parents work, a commitment to being equal partners in parenting, and of actually sharing in both the responsibilities and the sacrifice, is something that costs nothing.

I don't want to paint too pretty a picture of home or of work. At home we often squabble about which one of us needs to work while the other puts our son to bed. And at work, it's not as if editors meander through the newsroom ordering working parents to head home for dinner. All of the progress I have mentioned here has been born of conflict.

The uncharted frontier is now this: are men willing to make the same kinds of adjustments at work as women are making? How many journalists who are fathers ask to work four-day weeks or share jobs? How many pass up assignments that require extensive travel? How many men take the full paternity leave they're allowed? I wager that the answer is very few. And until they do, balancing work and family will continue to be seen, in journalism and in every other job, as a woman's issue.

The day when the capacity to balance work and family is seen as a notable achievement, a valuable talent, and a mark of machismo, is the day that the "mommy track"ends for good.